Controlling Your Pests

"A Life Worth Living Series"

Controlling Your Pests

Ridding Your Life of Bad Habits

Ross Brodfuehrer

COLLEGE PRESS
PUBLISHING COMPANY
Joplin, Missouri

Lessons are numbered Week 18 to Week 28, consistent with use as a
sequel to *Charting Your Course* and *Taking Out the Garbage*, but this book
may be used by itself, even if you have not gone through the earlier
books.

International Standard Book Number (ISBN): 0-89900-838-0

TO THE READER

They bite.   They buzz
    They creep.   They crawl.
    They swarm.   They sting.
    They chew.   They gnaw.

Some even suck your blood!
All distract you from what is good.
What are they?
Pests.

Cockroaches of criticism.   Wasps of worry.
    Spiders of procrastination.   Mice of mediocrity.
Rats of rebellion.   Stinkbugs of impurity.
And that ain't all!

Are you infested? If so, how badly? Will a small can of repellent be sufficient? Or do you need to call for professional-strength help?

Whatever it takes, begin today.
Pests only get worse.
Unchecked, they multiply.

But be warned.
Some of the pests, you have made into *pets*!
You raised them from eggs to adulthood in the ant farm of your sinful desires. And sticking your nose into this book may be like walking into a hornet's nest, one you helped form over the years from the mud and sticks of a worldly mind.

But have no fear!
And have no mercy!
Knock the nests down!

Drop the bug bomb of Holy Scripture into the confines of your pest-infested heart. Flip on the light switch of truth in the dark recesses of your soul and watch the vermin bug out!

You'll be glad you did.

Acknowledgments

At the risk of being a pest by way of repitition . . . thanks again to the same people acknowledged in Book One: Deena Kuhl for her meticulous editing and ongoing counsel (like a fly on flypaper); and the ladybugs who typed the proofs for all the books in this series: Nancy Beasy, Dottie Koebel, Holly Koebel, Detrick and Ellen Wokensperg. May you live long, fly high, sleep tight, and not let the bed bugs bite.

TAMING THE TONGUE

Criticism

D o you remember the famous line from the movie *Crocodile Dundee*? Dundee and his girlfriend are confronted by inner-city hooligans demanding his money. His girlfriend tells Dundee to give the cash because the gang leader has a knife.

Dundee responds, "That's not a knife. *That's* a knife," and pulls out his 15-inch backwoods blade. The punks quickly scatter.

Do you carry a knife? A pocketknife? Penknife? Keychain knife?

I can tell you that you do carry a knife — a knife at least as dangerous as Dundee's, and probably more so. It is your tongue. With it, we can slice and dice with the best of the electric turkey carvers. And unlike the steel variety, the tongue knife grows sharper with use.

The Bible says, "The tongue . . . is a fire, a world of evil among the parts of the body. . . . It is a restless evil, full of deadly poison. With the tongue we praise our Lord and Father, and with it we curse men . . . . My brothers, this should not be!" (James 3:6,8-10).

If you were to recall your most painful experience in life, it is doubtful that it was an illness or accident; it was more likely to be a deep cut from the verbal knife of someone you loved and respected. Maybe it was the time the coach called you a baboon, or your mom said that she wished you had never been born.

Arrests for physical assault are made every day, but few ever go on trial for verbal muggings. We must stop ourselves. Let's see how this week.

MONDAY

FOCUS:
Lord, this is a difficult, and probably convicting, topic. Help me to be open to any surgery You may want to perform on me.

Put Matthew 7:1-2 in your own words. **"Do not judge, or you too will be judged. For in the same way you judge others, you will be judged, and with the measure you use, it will be measured to you."**

On what basis do you usually judge people? Which areas are most critical?

❏ messy house
❏ lazy lifestyle
❏ ugly looks
❏ slow driving

❏ timid nature
❏ flashy clothes
❏ funny accent
❏ low intelligence

❏ other _____

If you are unsure about the areas in which you are judgmental, list three or four things that have made you angry in the past couple of days: your child's poor dress habits; your husband getting home late; your wife talking too much; devotion too hard . . .

🐜 _____

🐜 _____

🐜 _____

🐜 _____

With whom are you often angry? Put their name(s) in the space above as well.

PRAYER:
Lord, if You were to judge me on the basis of these same criteria, how would I fare?

FOCUS:
Father, surgery can be healing and healthy, though painful at the same time. Thank You that Your operations always leave us with more life than when we started.

What do you think is the lesson of Luke 18:9-14?

⁹To some who were confident of their own righteousness and looked down on everybody else, Jesus told this parable: ¹⁰"Two men went up to the temple to pray, one a Pharisee and the other a tax collector. ¹¹The Pharisee stood up and prayed about himself: 'God, I thank you that I am not like other men—robbers, evildoers, adulterers—or even like this tax collector. ¹²I fast twice a week and give a tenth of all I get.'

¹³"But the tax collector stood at a distance. He would not even look up to heaven, but beat his breast and said, 'God, have mercy on me, a sinner.'

¹⁴"I tell you that this man, rather than the other, went home justified before God. For everyone who exalts himself will be humbled, and he who humbles himself will be exalted."

Lesson: _____

_____

_____

_____

_____

_____

The Pharisees had certain rules. If a person obeyed these rules adequately, they were considered acceptable. If they violated the rules, they were considered unworthy of love and attention. Such rules are not only legalistic; they also are unfair. Look at Matthew 23:23-24.

²³"Woe to you, teachers of the law and Pharisees, you hypocrites! You give a tenth of your spices—mint, dill and cummin. But you have neglected the more important matters of the law—justice, mercy and faithfulness. You should have practiced the latter, without neglecting the former. ²⁴You blind guides! You strain out a gnat but swallow a camel."

Why did Jesus "woe" the Pharisees?

_____

_____

_____

Are you Pharisaical? Most of us are to some degree. We major in minors and minor in majors. We have hidden rules by which we judge others — rules that have little to do with true righteousness.

What rules have you emphasized most with those closest to you (children, spouse, students, co-workers)?

❑ looking good
❑ being good

❑ giving 10 percent
❑ giving the heart

❑ using proper English
❑ saying kind things

❑ don't embarrass the family
❑ obey the Lord, no matter what

PRAYER:
With God's help, list four of the most important rules to you, by which you have lived your life (and criticized others).

1. _____

2. _____

3. _____

4. _____

WEDNESDAY

FOCUS:
Who was the last person you saw before starting the devotion today? Did you see them through your eyes or the Father's eyes?

How "glorious" are you by the standard of Proverbs 19:11? **"A man's wisdom gives him patience; it is to his glory to overlook an offense."**

❑ very   ❑ some
❑ little   ❑ none

Which admonition do you most need of those in Romans 12:14-21? Underline it.

> **¹⁴Bless those who persecute you; bless and do not curse. ¹⁵Rejoice with those who rejoice; mourn with those who mourn. ¹⁶Live in harmony with one another. Do not be proud, but be willing to associate with people of low position. Do not be conceited.**
>
> **¹⁷Do not repay anyone evil for evil. Be careful to do what is right in the eyes of everybody. ¹⁸If it is possible, as far as it depends on you, live at peace with everyone. ¹⁹Do not take revenge, my friends, but leave room for God's wrath, for it is written: "It is mine to avenge; I will repay," says the Lord. ²⁰On the contrary:**
>
> > **"If your enemy is hungry, feed him;**
> > **if he is thirsty, give him something to drink.**
> > **In doing this, you will heap burning coals on his head."**
>
> **²¹Do not be overcome by evil, but overcome evil with good.**

Who is supposed to do the repaying for evil? _____

When you criticize, you become the lawmaker, the police, the judge, the prosecuting attorney, the jury, and the hangman all at once! Whose role have you been usurping?

_____

Think of a person who is constantly critical of others. Name that person.

_____

Is this person generally . . .

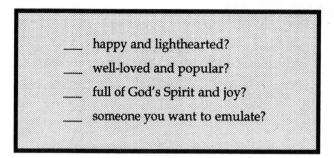

_____ happy and lighthearted?

_____ well-loved and popular?

_____ full of God's Spirit and joy?

_____ someone you want to emulate?

When you are critical of someone, even behind the person's back, what happens in and to your heart?

PRAYER:
Help me not to be overcome with criticism, but overcome criticism with praise and love.

THURSDAY

FOCUS:
How does the Father see you right now — with a critical eye or a forgiving heart?
Which way do you want Him to see you as you come before Him?

What three adjectives would you use to describe yourself?

1. _____

2. _____

3. _____

Are any of these descriptive terms negative (fat, old, bald)? _____

Some people are never verbally critical of others, but constantly put themselves down. Do you have a name you often call yourself when you make a bad golf shot, a poor financial decision, or burn dinner? What do you say to yourself when you blow it?

"_____"

Sometimes we have ungodly rules for ourselves, rules that leave big openings for Satan to accuse us, defeat us, and coax us to give up on ourselves. What standards do you set for yourself?

____ If I am not perfect, I fail.

____ I should never make a mistake.

____ Hard work is the mark of a real man. If I'm not busy, I feel like a lazy bum.

____ I should have a beauty queen figure. If not, I'm nothing but ugly.

____ I've got to make more money than my brother does to stay on top.

____ _____

____ _____

____ _____

13

If you judge yourself, whose authority are you usurping again?

What do you learn from 1 Corinthians 4:3-5?

³I care very little if I am judged by you or by any human court; indeed, I do not even judge myself. ⁴My conscience is clear, but that does not make me innocent. It is the Lord who judges me. ⁵Therefore judge nothing before the appointed time; wait till the Lord comes. He will bring to light what is hidden in darkness and will expose the motives of men's hearts. At that time each will receive his praise from God.

_____

_____

Treat yourself the way Christ would treat you — the way you should treat others.

PRAYER:
I relinquish my judgeship to You, Lord.

FRIDAY

FOCUS:
Forgive all those with whom you have been in contact this week — family, friends, strangers, workmates, and even yourself.

We ought never to be critical, loosely condemning others by our standards. But the Bible does give us the leeway to correct. Criticism and correction are two different matters.

What are you commanded to do in Matthew 18:15-17?

> [15]"**If your brother sins against you, go and show him his fault, just between the two of you. If he listens to you, you have won your brother over.** [16]**But if he will not listen, take one or two others along, so that 'every matter may be established by the testimony of two or three witnesses.'** [17]**If he refuses to listen to them, tell it to the church; and if he refuses to listen even to the church, treat him as you would a pagan or a tax collector."**

_____

_____

_____

What would you say are some differences between criticism and correction? You may want to consider Galatians 6:1-5:

> [1]**Brothers, if someone is caught in a sin, you who are spiritual should restore him gently. But watch yourself, or you also may be tempted.** [2]**Carry each other's burdens, and in this way you will fulfill the law of Christ.** [3]**If anyone thinks he is something when he is nothing, he deceives himself.** [4]**Each one should test his own actions. Then he can take pride in himself, without comparing himself to somebody else,** [5]**for each one should carry his own load.**

and Ephesians 4:15 as well:

> **Instead, speaking the truth in love, we will in all things grow up into him who is the Head, that is, Christ.**

Criticism	Correction

Jesus confronted the Pharisees. We read about that earlier this week. Paul confronted Peter. Nathan confronted King David. Criticism usually arises out of anger or a superior attitude; correction arises out of humility and concern. Criticism is meant to knock the other person down; correction is meant to lift him up. Criticism is blurted out; correction is preceded by prayer. Criticism hurts both the criticized and the criticizer; correction strengthens both. Criticism is easy to say and ugly in result; correction is hard to do but beautiful in the end.

PRAYER:
May my tongue no longer be a sharp knife in Satan's hands, but a healing tool in Your service, dear loving Lord.

NOT NOW, MAYBE LATER

Procrastination

A re you a procrastinator? Check anything below that you are currently putting off; then score yourself.

___ laundry
___ dishes
___ car repair
___ visit to in-laws
___ writing a thank-you note
___ dusting
___ physical exercise
___ doctor's check-up
___ starting a diet
___ asking for a raise
___ confronting a relational problem
___ cleaning the basement
___ dental appointment
___ polishing the silver
___ initiating a savings program
___ being baptized
___ finishing a book you started
___ buying a graduation gift
___ returning to college
___ preparing tax forms
___ planning vacation
___ returning books to the library
___ going on a mission trip
___ spending more time with your child/spouse

___ TOTAL

If you scored:

21-24: It's surprising that you are even doing this devotion!

16-20: You are either really good at prioritizing and most of these things are not important to you, or procrastination is a problem for you.

11-15: You are like most people, putting off what you dislike and feeling guilty about it.

1-5: You are either lying or you are the most disliked person in your neighborhood.

MONDAY

FOCUS:
Lord, teach me to put first things first, and to keep them first.

All of us are procrastinators. We may not procrastinate about the same things, but we all put off what we do not enjoy. A man may wash the car weekly, but delay balancing the checkbook until it's impossible to unravel. A woman may never allow a dirty dish to clutter her countertop, but never get around to learning her next-door neighbor's name.

What are you frustrated about because you put it off continuously? Is there one area in which, time after time, you kick yourself for not getting to it earlier? If so, what is it?

Read Acts 24:1-27 and answer the following questions.

¹Five days later the high priest Ananias went down to Caesarea with some of the elders and a lawyer named Tertullus, and they brought their charges against Paul before the governor. ²When Paul was called in, Tertullus presented his case before Felix: "We have enjoyed a long period of peace under you, and your foresight has brought about reforms in this nation. ³Everywhere and in every way, most excellent Felix, we acknowledge this with profound gratitude. ⁴But in order not to weary you further, I would request that you be kind enough to hear us briefly.

⁵"We have found this man to be a troublemaker, stirring up riots among the Jews all over the world. He is a ringleader of the Nazarene sect ⁶and even tried to desecrate the temple; so we seized him. ⁸By examining him yourself you will be able to learn the truth about all these charges we are bringing against him."

⁹The Jews joined in the accusation, asserting that these things were true.

¹⁰When the governor motioned for him to speak, Paul replied: "I know that for a number of years you have been a judge over this nation; so I gladly make my defense. ¹¹You can easily verify that no more than twelve days ago I went up to Jerusalem to worship. ¹²My accusers did not find me arguing with anyone at the temple, or stirring up a crowd in the synagogues or any-

18

where else in the city. [11]And they cannot prove to you the charges they are now making against me. [14]However, I admit that I worship the God of our fathers as a follower of the Way, which they call a sect. I believe everything that agrees with the Law and that is written in the Prophets, [15]and I have the same hope in God as these men, that there will be a resurrection of both the righteous and the wicked. [16]So I strive always to keep my conscience clear before God and man.

[17]"After an absence of several years, I came to Jerusalem to bring my people gifts for the poor and to present offerings. [18]I was ceremonially clean when they found me in the temple courts doing this. There was no crowd with me, nor was I involved in any disturbance. [19]But there are some Jews from the province of Asia, who ought to be here before you and bring charges if they have anything against me. [20]Or these who are here should state what crime they found in me when I stood before the Sanhedrin—[21]unless it was this one thing I shouted as I stood in their presence: 'It is concerning the resurrection of the dead that I am on trial before you today.'"

[22]Then Felix, who was well acquainted with the Way, adjourned the proceedings. "When Lysias the commander comes," he said, "I will decide your case." [23]He ordered the centurion to keep Paul under guard but to give him some freedom and permit his friends to take care of his needs.

[24]Several days later Felix came with his wife Drusilla, who was a Jewess. He sent for Paul and listened to him as he spoke about faith in Christ Jesus. [25]As Paul discoursed on righteousness, self-control and the judgment to come, Felix was afraid and said, "That's enough for now! You may leave. When I find it convenient, I will send for you." [26]At the same time he was hoping that Paul would offer him a bribe, so he sent for him frequently and talked with him.

[27]When two years had passed, Felix was succeeded by Porcius Festus, but because Felix wanted to grant a favor to the Jews, he left Paul in prison.

Why did Felix leave Paul in prison? _____
_____
_____

Who did Felix's procrastination affect and to what degree? _____
_____
_____

When it comes to your area of procrastination, answer the same questions. Why do you put it off? _____
_____
_____

Would you say your motive was: _____ selfish? _____ altruistic?

Who does your procrastination affect and to what degree? _____

_____

_____

PRAYER:
Do you need to repent? If so, do it now.

(Yes, now!)

 FOCUS:
Thank You, Lord, that You never procrastinate in forgiving me.

"Never put off until tomorrow what you can put off till next week!"

Is this humorous principle one by which you live? Think about it. Do you put things off as long as you possibly can, until they absolutely cannot wait any longer?

___ usually ___ sometimes ___ never

How does one stop procrastinating? How does one stop procrastinating stopping procrastinating?

One way is to see the reason why we delay and look at the results of doing so. What is the message of Proverbs 6:6-11?

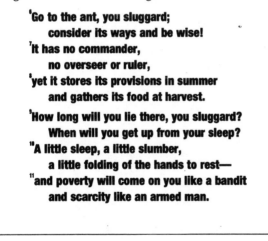

[6]Go to the ant, you sluggard;
 consider its ways and be wise!
[7]It has no commander,
 no overseer or ruler,
[8]yet it stores its provisions in summer
 and gathers its food at harvest.
[9]How long will you lie there, you sluggard?
 When will you get up from your sleep?
[10]A little sleep, a little slumber,
 a little folding of the hands to rest—
[11]and poverty will come on you like a bandit
 and scarcity like an armed man.

_____

_____

_____

_____

There are many reasons we put things off: We dislike it ("I hate cleaning."); we dislike with whom we must do it ("I hate cleaning because mother always tries to help."); we feel it won't make any difference ("I can clean the house, and it will be dirty again in 30 minutes!"); we fear it won't be done perfectly ("Once I start cleaning, there's no end. Why start?").

Choose one area in which you regularly procrastinate and jot down why.

❖ _____

What are the results of your procrastination? Possible poverty? Guilt feelings? The job becomes harder because of your delay?

◆ _____   ◆ _____
◆ _____   ◆ _____

PRAYER:
Prayerfully read Proverbs 6:6-11 again in view of what you put off.

FOCUS:
What sin have you procrastinated confessing to the Lord?
Air it out with Him now.

Moses endured some real hardships and challenges to lead the people out of Egypt. What was he looking forward to, according to Hebrews 11:24-28?

> **²⁴By faith Moses, when he had grown up, refused to be known as the son of Pharaoh's daughter. ²⁵He chose to be mistreated along with the people of God rather than to enjoy the pleasures of sin for a short time. ²⁶He regarded disgrace for the sake of Christ as of greater value than the treasures of Egypt, because he was looking ahead to his reward. ²⁷By faith he left Egypt, not fearing the king's anger; he persevered because he saw him who is invisible. ²⁸By faith he kept the Passover and the sprinkling of blood, so that the destroyer of the firstborn would not touch the firstborn of Israel.**

☆ _____

Hebrews 11 is called the "Hall of Faith" because it details many who did outstanding and difficult feats because they looked forward to the end result, the reward. Get out your Bible and list some of the things people did by faith in this chapter.

☆ _____   ☆ _____
☆ _____   ☆ _____
☆ _____   ☆ _____
☆ _____   ☆ _____
☆ _____   ☆ _____

Circle why Jesus endured the cross, according to Hebrews 12:2?

> **Let us fix our eyes on Jesus, the author and perfecter of our faith, who for the joy set before him endured the cross, scorning its shame, and sat down at the right hand of the throne of God.**

To stop procrastinating, get a clear vision of the end result. Take one troublesome yet important task you have been putting off and note some of the rewards you would have if you completed it. Don't forget rewards like relief from guilt, glorifying God, or a greater sense of success over your procrastination problem.

☆ _____

☆ _____

☆ _____

☆ _____

☆ _____

THURSDAY

FOCUS:
Did you do anything yesterday that you had been putting off? If so, what are your rewards?

Is there a difference between procrastination and waiting on the Lord? In 1 Samuel, Israel has asked for a king to lead them. God had the prophet Samuel find Saul and privately anoint him to be king. What do you learn about obedience and waiting on the Lord in 1 Samuel 10?

¹Then Samuel took a flask of oil and poured it on Saul's head and kissed him, saying, "Has not the Lᴏʀᴅ anointed you leader over his inheritance? ²When you leave me today, you will meet two men near Rachel's tomb, at Zelzah on the border of Benjamin. They will say to you, 'The donkeys you set out to look for have been found. And now your father has stopped thinking about them and is worried about you. He is asking, "What shall I do about my son?"'

³"Then you will go on from there until you reach the great tree of Tabor. Three men going up to God at Bethel will meet you there. One will be carrying three young goats, another three loaves of bread, and another a skin of wine. ⁴They will greet you and offer you two loaves of bread, which you will accept from them.

⁵"After that you will go to Gibeah of God, where there is a Philistine outpost. As you approach the town, you will meet a procession of prophets coming down from the high place with lyres, tambourines, flutes and harps being played before them, and they will be prophesying. ⁶The Spirit of the Lᴏʀᴅ will come upon you in power, and you will prophesy with them; and you will be changed into a different person. ⁷Once these signs are fulfilled, do whatever your hand finds to do, for God is with you.

⁸"Go down ahead of me to Gilgal. I will surely come down to you to sacrifice burnt offerings and fellowship offerings, but you must wait seven days until I come to you and tell you what you are to do."

⁹As Saul turned to leave Samuel, God changed Saul's heart, and all these signs were fulfilled that day. ¹⁰When they arrived at Gibeah, a procession of prophets met him; the Spirit of God came upon him in power, and he joined in their prophesying. ¹¹When all those who had formerly known him saw him prophesying with the prophets, they asked each other, "What is this that has happened to the son of Kish? Is Saul also among the prophets?"

¹²A man who lived there answered, "And who is their father?" So it became a saying: "Is Saul also among the prophets?" ¹³After Saul stopped prophesying, he went to the high place.

¹⁴Now Saul's uncle asked him and his servant, "Where have you been?"

"Looking for the donkeys," he said. "But when we saw they were not to be found, we went to Samuel."

¹⁵Saul's uncle said, "Tell me what Samuel said to you."

¹⁶Saul replied, "He assured us that the donkeys had been found." But he did not tell his uncle what Samuel had said about the kingship.

¹⁷Samuel summoned the people of Israel to the LORD at Mizpah ¹⁸and said to them, "This is what the LORD, the God of Israel, says: 'I brought Israel up out of Egypt, and I delivered you from the power of Egypt and all the kingdoms that oppressed you.' ¹⁹But you have now rejected your God, who saves you out of all your calamities and distresses. And you have said, 'No, set a king over us.' So now present yourselves before the LORD by your tribes and clans."

²⁰When Samuel brought all the tribes of Israel near, the tribe of Benjamin was chosen. ²¹Then he brought forward the tribe of Benjamin, clan by clan, and Matri's clan was chosen. Finally Saul son of Kish was chosen. But when they looked for him, he was not to be found. ²²So they inquired further of the LORD, "Has the man come here yet?"

And the LORD said, "Yes, he has hidden himself among the baggage."

²³They ran and brought him out, and as he stood among the people he was a head taller than any of the others. ²⁴Samuel said to all the people, "Do you see the man the LORD has chosen? There is no one like him among all the people."

Then the people shouted, "Long live the king!"

²⁵Samuel explained to the people the regulations of the kingship. He wrote them down on a scroll and deposited it before the LORD. Then Samuel dismissed the people, each to his own home.

²⁶Saul also went to his home in Gibeah, accompanied by valiant men whose hearts God had touched. ²⁷But some troublemakers said, "How can this fellow save us?" They despised him and brought him no gifts. But Saul kept silent.

I learned _____

_____

_____

_____

_____

_____

_____

Samuel gave Saul instructions both to wait (verse 8) and to act. He was to go a certain way home (by Rachel's tomb, then the tree at Tabor, then to Gibeah of God, and on to Gilgal).

Usually, waiting involves active obedience. In Acts 1:8, Jesus bids the disciples, "Do not leave Jerusalem, but wait for the gift my Father promised," that is, the power of the Holy Spirit which they later received on the day of Pentecost. But in that waiting period, we find the disciples active. They "all joined constantly together in prayer," (verse 14) and chose a replacement for Judas (verses 15-26).

Is there any area in which you are waiting on the Lord — a career change, a Christian mate, a place of service in the church? Name it.

PRAYER:
Are you actively waiting or sitting on your hands?
What is Jesus telling you to do while you wait?

FRIDAY

FOCUS:
"In the morning, O LORD, you hear my voice;
in the morning I lay my requests before you
and wait in expectation" (Psalm 5:3).

Is there a difference between procrastination and prioritizing? Why does Jesus delay coming to help His close friend Lazarus in John 11:1-44?

¹Now a man named Lazarus was sick. He was from Bethany, the village of Mary and her sister Martha. ²This Mary, whose brother Lazarus now lay sick, was the same one who poured perfume on the Lord and wiped his feet with her hair. ³So the sisters sent word to Jesus, "Lord, the one you love is sick."

⁴When he heard this, Jesus said, "This sickness will not end in death. No, it is for God's glory so that God's Son may be glorified through it." ⁵Jesus loved Martha and her sister and Lazarus. ⁶Yet when he heard that Lazarus was sick, he stayed where he was two more days.

⁷Then he said to his disciples, "Let us go back to Judea."

⁸"But Rabbi," they said, "a short while ago the Jews tried to stone you, and yet you are going back there?"

⁹Jesus answered, "Are there not twelve hours of daylight? A man who walks by day will not stumble, for he sees by this world's light. ¹⁰It is when he walks by night that he stumbles, for he has no light."

¹¹After he had said this, he went on to tell them, "Our friend Lazarus has fallen asleep; but I am going there to wake him up."

¹²His disciples replied, "Lord, if he sleeps, he will get better." ¹³Jesus had been speaking of his death, but his disciples thought he meant natural sleep.

¹⁴So then he told them plainly, "Lazarus is dead, ¹⁵and for your sake I am glad I was not there, so that you may believe. But let us go to him."

¹⁶Then Thomas (called Didymus) said to the rest of the disciples, "Let us also go, that we may die with him."

¹⁷On his arrival, Jesus found that Lazarus had already been in the tomb for four days. ¹⁸Bethany was less than two miles from Jerusalem, ¹⁹and many Jews had come to Martha and Mary to comfort them in the loss of their brother. ²⁰When Martha heard that Jesus was coming, she went out to meet him, but Mary stayed at home.

²¹"Lord," Martha said to Jesus, "if you had been here, my brother would not have died. ²²But I know that even now God will give you whatever you ask."

²³Jesus said to her, "Your brother will rise again."

²⁴Martha answered, "I know he will rise again in the resurrection at the last day."

[25]Jesus said to her, "I am the resurrection and the life. He who believes in me will live, even though he dies; [26]and whoever lives and believes in me will never die. Do you believe this?"

[27]"Yes, Lord," she told him, "I believe that you are the Christ, the Son of God, who was to come into the world."

[28]And after she had said this, she went back and called her sister Mary aside. "The Teacher is here," she said, "and is asking for you." [29]When Mary heard this, she got up quickly and went to him. [30]Now Jesus had not yet entered the village, but was still at the place where Martha had met him. [31]When the Jews who had been with Mary in the house, comforting her, noticed how quickly she got up and went out, they followed her, supposing she was going to the tomb to mourn there.

[32]When Mary reached the place where Jesus was and saw him, she fell at his feet and said, "Lord, if you had been here, my brother would not have died."

[33]When Jesus saw her weeping, and the Jews who had come along with her also weeping, he was deeply moved in spirit and troubled. "Where have you laid him?" he asked.

"Come and see, Lord," they replied.

[35]Jesus wept.

[36]Then the Jews said, "See how he loved him!"

[37]But some of them said, "Could not he who opened the eyes of the blind man have kept this man from dying?"

[38]Jesus, once more deeply moved, came to the tomb. It was a cave with a stone laid across the entrance. [39]"Take away the stone," he said.

"But, Lord," said Martha, the sister of the dead man, "by this time there is a bad odor, for he has been there four days."

[40]Then Jesus said, "Did I not tell you that if you believed, you would see the glory of God?"

[41]So they took away the stone. Then Jesus looked up and said, "Father, I thank you that you have heard me. [42]I knew that you always hear me, but I said this for the benefit of the people standing here, that they may believe that you sent me."

[43]When he had said this, Jesus called in a loud voice, "Lazarus, come out!" [44]The dead man came out, his hands and feet wrapped with strips of linen, and a cloth around his face.

Jesus said to them, "Take off the grave clothes and let him go."

Why?

What do you think was most important to Jesus in this passage? If you are unsure, look at verses 4 and 40. Jesus' first priority was to glorify God. If that meant allowing His beloved Lazarus to die, so be it. Jesus wept over the incident but knew that Lazarus's death would end in good, not only for God, but for Lazarus and his whole family.

If you were Lazarus, would you regret having died and then being resurrected? If you were Martha, would you wish you had not seen such a miracle? Their faith, perspective on life, and closeness of relationship had to have been increased tenfold by the experience.

List five things you have to do today.

1. _____

2. _____

3. _____

4. _____

5. _____

Prayerfully prioritize them according to this one question: What will most glorify God?

PRAYER:
Lord, help me to seek first Your glory and be satisfied.

I DESERVE BETTER!

Complaining

What can ruin a beautiful family Thanksgiving meal? One relative who complains about everything.

What can dampen a sunny Florida vacation at the beach? One child for whom nothing is fun enough.

What can make your dream job miserable? One boss who finds fault at every turn.

What can make any day a dud? Complaining.

Complaining has power. Awesome power. Power to paint a rainbow black, or a smile into a frown. Power to kill the dance at the wedding reception or murder the pop of a marvelous party.

Complaining has power. Power to take the gifts God Almighty gives and break them into pieces, like a spoiled child with an unsatisfactory birthday toy.

Complaining is man's lunar eclipse across God's good sun; grumbling drops the curtain on the Lord's outstanding play; griping spraypaints graffiti on God's masterpiece.

Complaining can take any good thing, even the best thing, and cast it into the mudhole called "not enough," belittle it, and siphon all its goodness.

Complaining is the visegrip that squeezes all the juice out of life's oranges, then wonders why all it has left are lemons. Grumbling crushes our piece of the daily bread and wonders why all it ever gets is the heel.

Complaining throws mud on what it has, then complains that what it has is dirty — then, out of resentment, throws the same dirt on whatever anyone else has.

What a stupid way to live! Don't fall for this trap of the Tempter.

MONDAY

FOCUS:
Lord, do I usually complain in prayer or praise in prayer?

What do you complain about most often?

___ weather	___ traffic
___ sports teams	___ wife
___ in-laws	___ husband
___ children	___ your house
___ health	___ clothes
___ money	___ other _____

What has your complaining produced for you in these areas? Name some ways it has paid off.

☆ _____   ☆ _____

☆ _____   ☆ _____

How well would you say you follow the command of Philippians 2:14-15 on this one-to-ten scale?

"Do everything without complaining or arguing, "so that you may become blameless and pure, children of God without fault in a crooked and depraved generation, in which you shine like stars in the universe . . . .

| 1 | 2 | 3 | 4 | 5 | 6 | 7 | 8 | 9 | 10 |

Paul wrote this letter from prison, locked up for innocently preaching the truth of Jesus. He had reason to complain. Circle what he recommends in 4:4.

'Rejoice in the Lord always. I will say it again: Rejoice!

Write verses 12-13 on a card and carry it with you all day.

> [12]I know what it is to be in need, and I know what it is to have plenty. I have learned the secret of being content in any and every situation, whether well fed or hungry, whether living in plenty or in want. [13]I can do everything through him who gives me strength.

Commit to rejoicing internally and audibly in every circumstance you enter today.

PRAYER:
Rejoice!

FOCUS:
Rejoice again!

Did you rejoice in every situation yesterday?

_____ Yes   _____ So-so   _____ No

If you did rejoice more than usual, what difference (if any) did it make in . . .

your disposition: _____

_____

those you met: _____

_____

your relationship with God: _____

_____

What was the basis of the man's complaint in Luke 12:13? **(Someone in the crowd said to Him, "Teacher, tell my brother to divide the inheritance with me.")**

_____

If he really was cheated, does he have a right to complain?

_____ Certainly   _____ Maybe   _____ Not at all

Why will Jesus not help the man, and what is the meaning of the Lord's answer?

"Jesus replied, "Man, who appointed me a judge or an arbiter between you?" "Then he said to them, "Watch out! Be on your guard against all kinds of greed; a man's life does not consist in the abundance ofhis possessions."

_____

_____

_____

_____

We tend to complain about what is most important to us. Considering what you generally express dissatisfaction about, what is most important to you?

1. _____

2. _____

3. _____

↑
What does it say about you?

 PRAYER:
Lord, if I were to complain, with what would You want me to be dissatisfied?

FOCUS:
Father, do You have any complaint against me just now?

Read 2 Kings 6:8-23, and answer the questions.

⁸Now the king of Aram was at war with Israel. After conferring with his officers, he said, "I will set up my camp in such and such a place."

⁹The man of God sent word to the king of Israel: "Beware of passing that place, because the Arameans are going down there." ¹⁰So the king of Israel checked on the place indicated by the man of God. Time and again Elisha warned the king, so that he was on his guard in such places.

¹¹This enraged the king of Aram. He summoned his officers and demanded of them, "Will you not tell me which of us is on the side of the king of Israel?"

¹²"None of us, my lord the king," said one of his officers, "but Elisha, the prophet who is in Israel, tells the king of Israel the very words you speak in your bedroom."

¹³"Go, find out where he is," the king ordered, "so I can send men and capture him." The report came back: "He is in Dothan." ¹⁴Then he sent horses and chariots and a strong force there. They went by night and surrounded the city.

¹⁵When the servant of the man of God got up and went out early the next morning, an army with horses and chariots had surrounded the city. "Oh, my lord, what shall we do?" the servant asked.

¹⁶"Don't be afraid," the prophet answered. "Those who are with us are more than those who are with them."

¹⁷And Elisha prayed, "O LORD, open his eyes so he may see." Then the LORD opened the servant's eyes, and he looked and saw the hills full of horses and chariots of fire all around Elisha.

¹⁸As the enemy came down toward him, Elisha prayed to the LORD, "Strike these people with blindness." So he struck them with blindness, as Elisha had asked.

¹⁹Elisha told them, "This is not the road and this is not the city. Follow me, and I will lead you to the man you are looking for." And he led them to Samaria.

²⁰After they entered the city, Elisha said, "LORD, open the eyes of these men so they can see." Then the LORD opened their eyes and they looked, and there they were, inside Samaria.

²¹When the king of Israel saw them, he asked Elisha, "Shall I kill them, my father? Shall I kill them?"

²²"Do not kill them," he answered. "Would you kill men you have captured with your own sword or bow? Set food and water before them so that they may eat and drink and then go back to their master." ²³So he prepared a great feast for them, and after they had finished eating and drinking, he sent them away, and they returned to their master. So the bands from Aram stopped raiding Israel's territory.

1. Who was Elisha? _____

2. Why did the king of Aram want to capture him? _____

_____

_____

3. In verse 15, what is the servant's concern? _____

_____

_____

4. What does Elisha pray for the servant? _____

When you complain, could it be that you are not seeing the whole picture? Take one area of common complaint for you, and ask God to open your eyes to see His perspective on it. Jot any thoughts down below.

PRAYER:
Praise God for Romans 8:31 —

"If God is for us, who can be against us?"

37

THURSDAY

FOCUS:
Thank God for something for which you have not thanked Him in a long time.

Complaining is often an expression of two things:

1. a lack of trust in God. "He can't or won't take care of me the way I deserve."

2. a feeling that our rights have been violated. "I deserve a pretty wife, a kind husband, a new car, a bigger house."

What do you like best from Isaiah 40:27-31?

> ²⁷Why do you say, O Jacob,
>   and complain, O Israel,
> "My way is hidden from the Lᴏʀᴅ;
>   my cause is disregarded by my God?"
> ²⁸Do you not know?
>   Have you not heard?
> The Lᴏʀᴅ is the everlasting God,
>   the Creator of the ends of the earth.
> He will not grow tired or weary,
>   and His understanding no one can fathom.
> ²⁹He gives strength to the weary
>   and increases the power of the weak.
> ³⁰Even youths grow tired and weary,
>   and young men stumble and fall;
> ³¹but those who hope in the Lᴏʀᴅ
>   will renew their strength.
> They will soar on wings like eagles;
>   they will run and not grow weary,
>   they will walk and not be faint.

I like: _____

Do you believe this passage?

ALL   –   MOST   –   SOME   –   A LITTLE

First Corinthians 10:10 is about the people of Israel after they have been miraculously freed from slavery in Egypt. In one sentence, what is your reaction to this verse?

And do not grumble, as some of them did—and were killed by the destroying angel.

"_____

_____"

Grumbling is not just a minor infraction in God's justice system, especially when it is grumbling against God (which is what most grumbling is, when you come right down to it).

How would you characterize David's attitude toward God in 2 Samuel 7:18-19?

Then King David went in and sat before the LORD, and he said:
"Who am I, O Sovereign LORD, and what is my family, that you have brought me this far? And as if this were not enough in your sight, O Sovereign LORD, you have also spoken about the future of the house of your servant. Is this your usual way of dealing with man, O Sovereign LORD?

 Write the first three words of David's prayer, then write your own prayer to God.

_____

_____

_____

_____

_____

_____

FRIDAY

FOCUS:
Father, show me today how and where I may complain.

Should we ever gripe? Should we always be Miss Polyanna Positive? Jesus wasn't. Matthew 23 is a diatribe against the Pharisees. In Matthew 17:17 He complained about the hardness of the people, saying, "O unbelieving and perverse generation, how long shall I put up with you?"

What is the gist of what King David writes in Psalm 142:1-2 (the same king who prayed the "who am I?" prayer we studied yesterday)?

¹**I cry aloud to the LORD; I lift up my voice to the LORD for mercy. ²I pour out my complaint before him; before him I tell my trouble.**

_____

_____

Could it be that there is a difference between complaining because you like to complain, and complaining out of sincere need, righteous indignation, or in faith God will change things?

Decide two or three rules for yourself: how and when you will complain and how and when you will not.

1. _____

_____

_____

2. _____

_____

_____

3. _____

_____

_____

PRAYER:
Check these rules out with God.

40

LOSING SLEEP AND COUNTING SHEEP

Worry

A man once said, "Do not worry about tomorrow, for tomorrow will worry about itself." Is that true? Or is it pie-in-the-sky thinking?

The man who said that was not retired, was not independently wealthy, was not married, was not even employed.

The man who said that knew the future of the world rested squarely on His shoulders. He knew He had to start a revolution that would spread globally, and He had only a few short months to do so. He knew His few followers were uneducated, untrained, and not fully loyal. He knew He faced certain execution in less than three years.

"Don't worry." The man who said that is quoted in Matthew 6:34. The man who said that was Jesus Christ.

Amazing, when you think about it. Jesus had more to carry than anyone in history, yet He worried less than them all. He talked often of peace and trust. He was never in a hurry, never anxious, never rushing to appointments. He didn't bite His fingernails and eat a half gallon of chocolate chip ice cream to salve His fears. He didn't drink wine to calm His frayed nerves or take a cruise to escape the pressure.

Jesus did His work without worry, trusting fully in His Father in heaven. It sounds too simple. Why can't we do that?

Maybe we can! Jesus said those words to us. And He never told us to do anything that He did not also give us the power to obey.

So don't worry! Jesus can help you get over your worry!

MONDAY

FOCUS:
Lord, on a one-to-ten scale, how much would You say I need this study on worry?

Luke 10:38-42 tells of Jesus visiting the home of Martha and Mary. Before reading it, think about what you would have to do if Jesus were actually coming to stay at your house for a few days. Remember, He would be eating, sleeping, and teaching in your home. Not only that, but as usually was the case, wherever He went, a large group of people trooped along (hungry and thirsty, of course) as well as daily crowds of listeners (who often got a little hungry and thirsty as well!)

To Do List

Now read the passage.

³⁸**As Jesus and his disciples were on their way, he came to a village where a woman named Martha opened her home to him. ³⁹She had a sister called Mary, who sat at the Lord's feet listening to what he said. ⁴⁰But Martha was distracted by all the preparations that had to be made. She came to him and asked, "Lord, don't you care that my sister has left me to do the work by myself? Tell her to help me!"**

⁴¹**"Martha, Martha," the Lord answered, "you are worried and upset about many things, but only one thing is needed. Mary has chosen what is better, and it will not be taken away from her."**

Now decide which sister you are more like.

☐ Martha   ☐ Mary

Pray about the message of this passage, and write what you think it is.

_____

_____

_____

If Jesus were to speak verse 41 to you today, how would He finish it? Fill in the first blank with your name, and the others with your answers.

"_____, you are worried and upset about _____

_____

_____

but only one thing is needed, and it is _____."

PRAYER:
Will you follow the Lord's advice today?

TUESDAY

FOCUS:
Did you follow the Lord's advice yesterday? Ask Him.

In Matthew 6:25-34, about what are we told not to worry and about what are we told to be concerned?

[25]"Therefore I tell you, do not worry about your life, what you will eat or drink; or about your body, what you will wear. Is not life more important than food, and the body more important than clothes? [26]Look at the birds of the air; they do not sow or reap or store away in barns, and yet your heavenly Father feeds them. Are you not much more valuable than they? [27]Who of you by worrying can add a single hour to his life?

[28]"And why do you worry about clothes? See how the lilies of the field grow. They do not labor or spin. [29]Yet I tell you that not even Solomon in all his splendor was dressed like one of these. [30]If that is how God clothes the grass of the field, which is here today and tomorrow is thrown into the fire, will he not much more clothe you, O you of little faith? [31]So do not worry, saying, 'What shall we eat?' or 'What shall we drink?' or 'What shall we wear?' [32]For the pagans run after all these things, and your heavenly Father knows that you need them. [33]But seek first his kingdom and his righteousness, and all these things will be given to you as well. [34]Therefore do not worry about tomorrow, for tomorrow will worry about itself. Each day has enough trouble of its own."

Don't Worry	Be Concerned

Has there ever been a time when you did not have the things in the left-hand column? If so, what and when? _____

_____

_____

Were you obediently walking with the Lord at that time?

       ❑   Yes   ❑   No

What is promised in verse 33? _____

What is the condition of that promise? _____

What have you been seeking first?

☛ First thing in the morning: _____

☛ First check you write every month: _____

☛ First factor when making a decision: _____

☛ First act when you sit to eat: _____

☛ First thing you do on vacation: _____

 PRAYER:
What would have to change in your life for you to say honestly, "I seek first the kingdom and rule of God in my life"?

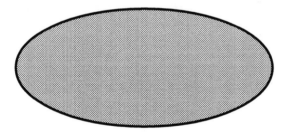

WEDNESDAY

FOCUS:
Cry out to God for someone less fortunate than yourself.

Write the first half of Proverbs 12:25 here:

_____

You have listed some of your worries already this week in this devotion. Now list them all. What really does eat at your mind and peace? What concerns do you turn over and over in your head? What gnaws at your stomach and chews at your nerves? What wakes you up at night or refuses to let you go to sleep? Is it money? Children? Chores? Parents? Sin? Love? Revenge? Failure? Success? Fear? Unfulfilled dreams?

Note all your worries below. Write them as quickly as you can, without a lot of thought.

Answer these questions in the form of a written prayer to God.
- **?** How much has worry helped you?
- **?** How much has it hurt you?
- **?** Is worry a good testimony for the Lord?
- **?** If you didn't worry, how much more energy, joy, laughter, and love would you have?
- **?** What keeps you from ceasing to worry?

Father in heaven,

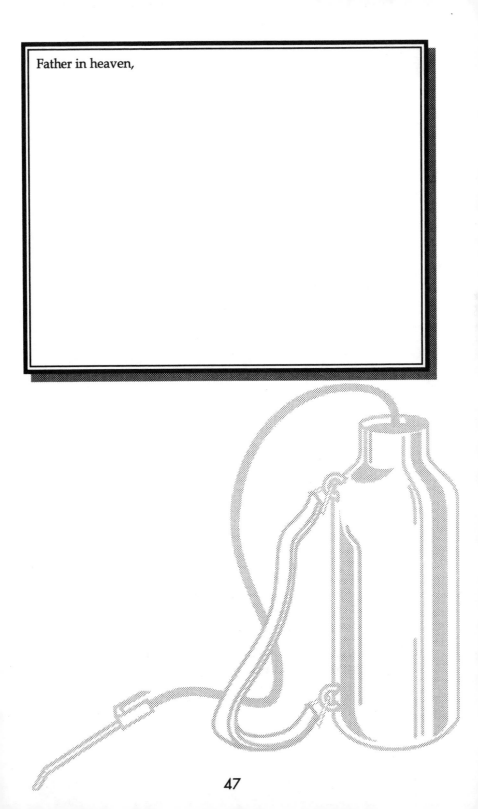

THURSDAY

FOCUS:
Pray for someone you know who is a "worry wart."

If over coffee one day, a friend came to you for advice on how to stop being so anxious all the time, what would you tell him or her?

If this friend said, "I want to know what the Bible says," how might you respond, using Philippians 4? List the verse and the advice.

Verse _____ Advice _____

Verse _____ Advice _____

Verse _____ Advice _____

Verse _____ Advice _____

Verse _____ Advice _____

Circle the advice you most need to hear yourself!

Notice that there is a difference between worry and concern. In verse 10, Paul is glad that the Christians at Philippi are concerned about him.

Here are some differences between worry and concern:

> Worry frets; concern takes action.

> Worry prays; concern prays and is confident of an answer.

> Worry shrinks back; concern marches forward boldly.

> Worry is primarily selfish ("Oh, poor me!"); concern is about others ("Poor John.").

> Worry saps your energy; concern charges your batteries.

 **PRAYER:**
Obey chapter 4:6-7.

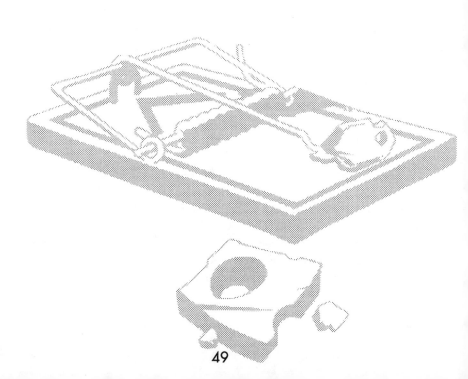

FRIDAY

FOCUS:
Obey Philippians 4:6-7 again!

> ⁶Do not be anxious about anything, but in everything, by prayer and petition, with thanksgiving, present your requests to God. ⁷And the peace of God, which transcends all understanding, will guard your hearts and your minds in Christ Jesus.

Should we worry about our relationship with God? Try to summarize Luke 12:4-7.

> ⁴"I tell you, my friends, do not be afraid of those who kill the body and after that can do no more. ⁵But I will show you whom you should fear: Fear him who, after the killing of the body, has power to throw you into hell. Yes, I tell you, fear him. ⁶Are not five sparrows sold for two pennies? Yet not one of them is forgotten by God. ⁷Indeed, the very hairs of your head are all numbered. Don't be afraid; you are worth more than many sparrows."

We are not to fear people at all. We are to fear Almighty God, because our ultimate and lasting destiny lies with Him. Yet we don't need to be afraid of Him because He values us highly. Look at verse 32. **"Do not be afraid, little flock, for your Father has been pleased to give you the kingdom."** Has that been your view of God's attitude toward your salvation, that He is pleased to give it to you?

_____ Yes   _____ No   _____ Never thought about it

If we have no worries about where we stand with God, what can be the focus and aim of our lives? See verse 33.

> "Sell your possessions and give to the poor. Provide purses for yourselves that will not wear out, a treasure in heaven that will not be exhausted, where no thief comes near and no moth destroys."

Verse 34 says, **"For where your treasure is, there your heart will be also."** Where is your treasure?

That is probably where your worries lie as well.

PRAYER:
Write below the things that really are your treasures in life.

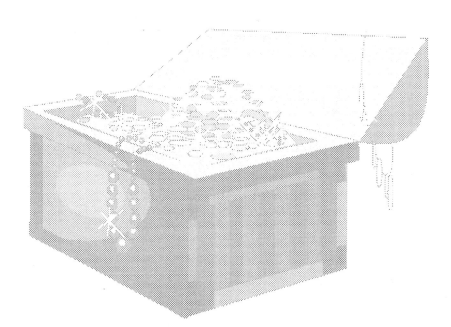

YOU'RE NOT A KID ANYMORE

Grow Up!

The apostle Paul writes in Ephesians 4:1, **"As a prisoner of the Lord, then, I urge you to live a life worthy of the calling you have received."**

It's one thing to feel called to become a brain surgeon. Living up to that calling would entail hours of study, practice, and discipline.

If our country called on you to become President of the United States, you would need to do more than take the oath of office to be a worthy head of state. Hard work, a knowledge of foreign affairs, daily vigilance would be required.

Do you know that you have a calling higher than that of chief surgeon? Greater than leader of the nation? You are named to be a child of the King of kings, an emissary for the Lord of lords, an agent in His Majesty's secret service.

We became Christians as a gift; we were chosen through no righteousness or expertise of our own. No one sweats their way into God's grace.

But once we are part of the royal family, the Father does call on us to begin to look like and act like a member of the family. We should begin to take on a family resemblance.

God has great expectations for you, plans for joys in your life, adventures year by year, impact on this world, representation of Him and His cause.

Live up to what He has for you. He will help you all the way.

FOCUS:
Pray for your family members to put Christ first.

Men, do you remember standing in front of the mirror as an adolescent, searching for enough facial hair to finally begin to shave, then getting your first razor, lathering up, and then cutting yourself with the blade? Yes! You had become a man! (Or at least you thought so.)

Ladies, do you remember your first car date, when dad finally allowed you to go out with a boy and mom helped you select your dress? After the school dance, you stood at your doorstep, and he kissed you. Yes! You were becoming a woman! (Or at least you thought so.)

When did you come of age? What experience pushed you over the hump to adulthood? Was it enrolling in college? The death of a parent? The wedding altar? When do you think you became a man or a woman?

What would you say maturity is, according to Ephesians 4:1-16?

¹**As a prisoner for the Lord, then, I urge you to live a life worthy of the calling you have received. ²Be completely humble and gentle; be patient, bearing with one another in love. ³Make every effort to keep the unity of the Spirit through the bond of peace. ⁴There is one body and one Spirit— just as you were called to one hope when you were called— ⁵one Lord, one faith, one baptism; ⁶one God and Father of all, who is over all and through all and in all.**

⁷**But to each one of us grace has been given as Christ apportioned it. ⁸This is why it says:**

"**When he ascended on high,
he led captives in his train
and gave gifts to men.**"

⁹**(What does "he ascended" mean except that he also descended to the lower, earthly regions? ¹⁰He who descended is the very one who ascended higher than all the heavens, in order to fill the whole universe.) ¹¹It was he who gave some to be apostles, some to be prophets, some to be evangelists, and some to be pastors and teachers, ¹²to prepare God's people for works of service, so that the body of Christ may be built up ¹³until we all reach unity in the faith**

and in the knowledge of the Son of God and become mature, attaining to the whole measure of the fullness of Christ.

¹⁴Then we will no longer be infants, tossed back and forth by the waves, and blown here and there by every wind of teaching and by the cunning and craftiness of men in their deceitful scheming. ¹⁵Instead, speaking the truth in love, we will in all things grow up into him who is the Head, that is, Christ. ¹⁶From him the whole body, joined and held together by every supporting ligament, grows and builds itself up in love, as each part does its work.

_____

_____

_____

When did you come of age in Christ? What pushed you over the edge from youth to adulthood? (or are you there yet)?

_____

_____

_____

PRAYER:
Are you willing to ask God to do what is necessary to mature you?

TUESDAY

FOCUS:
What are you worried about today? Give it to God.

Becoming a Christian is often called being born again, based on John 3:5,7: "I tell you the truth, no one can enter the kingdom of God unless he is born of water and the Spirit. . . . You must be born again."

Those who are born again often are called infants in the Scriptures. Ephesians 4:14 is an example.

> **Then we will no longer be infants, tossed back and forth by the waves, and blown here and there by every wind of teaching and by the cunning and craftiness of men in their deceitful scheming.**

List three or four characteristics of people at each life stage:

INFANCY:
(Example: Needs to be fed by others.)

✔ _____   ✔ _____
✔ _____   ✔ _____

CHILDHOOD:

✔ _____   ✔ _____
✔ _____   ✔ _____

ADOLESCENCE:

✔ _____   ✔ _____
✔ _____   ✔ _____

EARLY ADULTHOOD:

✔ _____   ✔ _____
✔ _____   ✔ _____

MATURE ADULTHOOD:

✔ _____   ✔ _____
✔ _____   ✔ _____

If you were to spiritualize each characteristic, for example, exchanging "unable to feed self" with "unable to feed self spiritually; unable to understand God's Word on my own," at what stage of spiritual development would you say you are? Circle the correct stage on page 55.

Read Ephesians 4:14-15.

> ¹⁴Then we will no longer be infants, tossed back and forth by the waves, and blown here and there by every wind of teaching and by the cunning and craftiness of men in their deceitful scheming. ¹⁵Instead, speaking the truth in love, we will in all things grow up into him who is the Head, that is, Christ.

What key change would you need to make in order to move up into the next stage of maturity?

PRAYER:
Lord, move me up one stage today!

WEDNESDAY

FOCUS:
At what spiritual life stage did you live yesterday?

Circle one:
Infancy – Childhood – Adolescence – Adulthood.

How many years did it take you to reach physical maturity? _____ years

Many Christians become impatient with their disappointingly slow spiritual development. They compare themselves with the battle-worn saint who has weathered the fight for 45 years, and come up woefully short.

Then the immature believers beat themselves up, and in doing so, actually lose some of the ground they had gained. Satan, the accuser of the brethren, wins a moral victory over them.

Spiritual development is just as slow, tenuous and trying as physical development. It will take time.

What encouragement do you find in Paul's words from Philippians 3:7-16? Circle it and summarize it below.

> [7] But whatever was to my profit I now consider loss for the sake of Christ. [8] What is more, I consider everything a loss compared to the surpassing greatness of knowing Christ Jesus my Lord, for whose sake I have lost all things. I consider them rubbish, that I may gain Christ [9] and be found in him, not having a righteousness of my own that comes from the law, but that which is through faith in Christ—the righteousness that comes from God and is by faith. [10] I want to know Christ and the power of his resurrection and the fellowship of sharing in his sufferings, becoming like him in his death, [11] and so, somehow, to attain to the resurrection from the dead.
>
> [12] Not that I have already obtained all this, or have already been made perfect, but I press on to take hold of that for which Christ Jesus took hold of me. [13] Brothers, I do not consider myself yet to have taken hold of it. But one thing I do: Forgetting what is behind and straining toward what is ahead, [14] I press on toward the goal to win the prize for which God has called me heavenward in Christ Jesus.
>
> [15] All of us who are mature should take such a view of things. And if on some point you think differently, that too God will make clear to you. [16] Only let us live up to what we have already attained.

_____

_____

_____

_____

Have you . . .

    ___   forgotten what lies behind?

    ___   focused on the prize?

    ___   considered worldly profit to be loss?

    ___   asked God to make it clear?

 PRAYER:
See Jesus Christ before you as you pray to Him today.

58

THURSDAY

FOCUS:
What worship does God deserve from you today?

What does it say about childish things in 1 Corinthians 13:11? **When I was a child, I talked like a child, I thought like a child, I reasoned like a child. When I became a man, I put childish ways behind me.**

_____

Some childish things can be simple fun — a sport, hobby, or following a favorite team. But childish things can also become tyrants, demanding our time and attention. To what childish things do you give too much attention?

____	TOYS: sports car, stereo system, computer gadgetry, woodworking shop, etc.
____	SPORTS: golf game, following favorite team, card club, etc.
____	DAYDREAMING: wishing you had a different spouse, job, house, family, even a different life
____	TRYING TO FIT IN: worrying over clothes, gaining proper status symbols, working to gain access to a certain group, etc.
____	PROTECTING YOUR STUFF: not sharing, hoarding, being afraid to let go of things, stockpiling, etc.
____	OTHER: _____

List some of the "mature" attitudes and actions from 1 Corinthians 13. Put those at which you do well above the line; put those in which you need some improvement below the line.

_____

PRAYER:
What are you going to do about today's lesson?

 FOCUS:
Praise God for everything that happened yesterday. (Yes, everything.)

Becoming mature is hard work. But you do not have to do it all yourself. You have an ally. Write the great promise of Philippians 1:6 in your own words: **Being confident of this, that He who began a good work in you will carry it on to completion until the day of Christ Jesus.**

_____

_____

_____

_____

Also write below what you think Philippians 2:12-13 means.

[12]Therefore, my dear friends, as you have always obeyed—not only in my presence, but now much more in my absence—continue to work out your salvation with fear and trembling, [13]for it is God who works in you to will and to act according to his good purpose.

_____

_____

_____

_____

If you fully believed these verses, what would change in your life?

1. _____

2. _____

3. _____

4. _____

Can you name some way that God has worked recently in your life? An answer to prayer? A stronger conviction over sin? More patience with children? Bolder witness at work? What has God done in you lately?

1. _____

2. _____

3. _____

4. _____

The key to godly growth is faith, trusting that Almighty God can and will grow you up to be a reflection of Jesus. Trust Him to be working, slowly but surely!

PRAYER:
Thank God for today's passages.

STANDING OUT IN THE CROWD

Be Distinctive

D istinctive:
"having a special quality, style, attractiveness; notable."

Could Webster's use your name to define "distinctive?"

"Oh, no, there is nothing special about me. I'm just a face in the crowd; I've never stood out."

If you are not distinctive, why not?

Is it because you feel unworthy of standing out?

Is it because you have been taught that it is sinful to draw attention to yourself?

Is it that you worry that if people noticed you, they also might criticize you?

Are you willing to be distinguished as being undistinguished?

"Yes, I'm different. I intend to keep being different. No way am I going to continue to be just a number, one of many, a carbon copy."

If you are different, what is it about you that glimmers? Is it . . .

Your colorful clothes?   Your money?   Your sick humor?

Your sky-high personality?   Your ox-like work ethic?

Is that the glimmer you want people to spot and focus upon? In Matthew 5 Jesus said,

[14]**"You** [yes, *you* who are reading this] **are the light of the world** [shiny, glimmering, attractive]. **A city on a hill cannot be hidden** [you have been built by the master carpenter]. [15]**Neither do people light a lamp and put it under a bowl** [nor set up a spotlight in the hall closet]. **Instead they put it on its stand, and it gives light to everyone in the house.** [16]**In the same way, let your light** [yes, you have distinctive light] **shine before men, that they may see your good deeds and praise your Father in heaven** [the ultimate purpose]."

You are of Christ.

Be distinctive!

FOCUS:
Lord, who do I look most like: My dad? My mom? My boss? My dog? The average American? You?

Ephesians 4:17 begins, **"So I tell you this, and insist on it in the Lord . . ."**

What are some of the things you insist upon in each role/place?

In your home: (Example: wipe your feet before entering, say something nice or say nothing at all, etc.)

🖎

🖎

🖎

🖎

🖎

At your workplace: (The customer is always right, make a profit, etc.)

☎

☎

☎

☎

☎

In your personal life: (Do my best, look good at all costs, etc.)

☞

☞

☞

☞

☞

Read Ephesians 4:17-32 and put in one sentence what you think it is saying.

^{17}So I tell you this, and insist on it in the Lord, that you must no longer live as the Gentiles do, in the futility of their thinking. ^{18}They are darkened in their understanding and separated from the life of God because of the ignorance that is in them due to the hardening of their hearts. ^{19}Having lost all sensitivity, they have given themselves over to sensuality so as to indulge in every kind of impurity, with a continual lust for more.

^{20}You, however, did not come to know Christ that way. ^{21}Surely you heard of him and were taught in him in accordance with the truth that is in Jesus. ^{22}You were taught, with regard to your former way of life, to put off your old self, which is being corrupted by its deceitful desires; ^{23}to be made new in the attitude of your minds; ^{24}and to put on the new self, created to be like God in true righteousness and holiness.

^{25}Therefore each of you must put off falsehood and speak truthfully to his neighbor, for we are all members of one body. ^{26}"In your anger do not sin": Do not let the sun go down while you are still angry, ^{27}and do not give the devil a foothold. ^{28}He who has been stealing must steal no longer, but must work, doing something useful with his own hands, that he may have something to share with those in need.

^{29}Do not let any unwholesome talk come out of your mouths, but only what is helpful for building others up according to their needs, that it may benefit those who listen. ^{30}And do not grieve the Holy Spirit of God, with whom you were sealed for the day of redemption. ^{31}Get rid of all bitterness, rage and anger, brawling and slander, along with every form of malice. ^{32}Be kind and compassionate to one another, forgiving each other, just as in Christ God forgave you.

_____

_____

How do the things you insist upon compare with what God insists upon? Give your reaction.

_____

_____

_____

_____

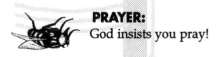

PRAYER:
God insists you pray!

64

TUESDAY

FOCUS:
Review yesterday and praise God for where you saw Him at work.

Yesterday you were asked to pray about whom you are most like. Now answer that question:

___ father	___ a friend
___ mother	___ a former boss/teacher
___ brother/sister	___ Jesus Christ

___ the average American Christian

Whom are we NOT supposed to live like, according to Ephesians 4:17? **So I tell you this, and insist on it in the Lord, that you must no longer live as the Gentiles [or pagans] do, in the futility of their thinking.**

List some ways Paul describes these people in vv. 17-19, page 64.

thinking is _____

understanding is _____

separated from _____

ignorance due to _____

lost all _____

given themselves over to _____

Would you . . .

___ follow a blind man on a mountain trail?

___ sit under the teaching of an imbecile?

___ emulate the lifestyle of a corpse?

___ follow the example of a convict?

Do you in some ways follow the patterns of a dead and dying, disgusted and disgusting, tired and tiring world? Is there any way in which you are tempted to follow the world's ways in any of these areas?

	Pagan Way	Christ's Way
Who is important:	❏	❏
Who is unimportant:	❏	❏
What makes life good:	❏	❏
Where your hope and strength lie:	❏	❏

 PRAYER:
Decide with God one way you will be more like Christ.

FOCUS:
Think of what Jesus Christ is like and acknowledge your beliefs to Him.

Paul wrote the book of Ephesians 2,000 years ago. Surely we have progressed and evolved for the better since then. Or have we? How well does verse 19 of chapter 4 (page 64) describe America?

____ a) not at all   ____ c) fairly closely

____ b) somewhat   ____ d) right on the money

Best-selling author Louis L'Amour, who was often asked why he didn't put more sex in his books, observed that "in our culture, sex is an ordeal, or it is rape, or an athletic endeavor. Nobody seems to be having any fun."

Let's contrast love and lust:

> Love gives; lust takes.
>
> Love seeks to satisfy another; lust seeks to gratify itself.
>
> Love wants the best for the other; lust merely wants.
>
> Love is satisfied with loving; lust is never satisfied for long.
>
> Love relishes simple pleasures over and over; lust craves something more exotic until no perversion is exotic enough.
>
> Love only needs one other; lust always needs someone else.
>
> Love has fun; lust thinks fun will be around the next corner.

If your marriage or other relationships seem dull and boring, try giving yourself instead of gratifying yourself. Try it for two days and see if it is "better to give than to receive."

PRAYER:
Examine with God whether you are a lover or a luster.

Then decide which one He is.

FOCUS:
What part of my culture around me should I be hating instead of desiring?

What is said about the "old self" and the "new self" in Ephesians 4:20-24?

²⁰You, however, did not come to know Christ that way. ²¹Surely you heard of him and were taught in him in accordance with the truth that is in Jesus. ²²You were taught, with regard to your former way of life, to put off your old self, which is being corrupted by its deceitful desires; ²³to be made new in the attitude of your minds; ²⁴and to put on the new self, created to be like God in true righteousness and holiness.

OLD SELF   NEW SELF

What difference has Christ made in your life? What were you like before you truly surrendered to Him? How are you changed now?

OLD SELF   NEW SELF

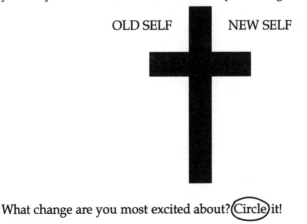

What change are you most excited about? Circle it!

What was your first big change as a believer? Box it.

What change is the latest one? Star ✱it.

What change do you most need now to be the divine representative Christ wants you to be?

Notice that our sinful urges are called "deceitful desires" in verse 22. What payoff does the world or Satan promise you for *not* changing what you put in the circle above and keeping up "old self" practices?

_____

Will those promises really pay off, or are they deceitful?

| _____ fulfilling | _____ deceitful |

PRAYER:
Pray for "new self" change.

FRIDAY

FOCUS:
"Every morning your mercies are new." Confess your "old self" shortcomings as sin and receive God's full and unrestricted forgiveness. Be new!

Ephesians 4:25-32 contrasts the practices of the old and new selves.

> ²⁵Therefore each of you must put off falsehood and speak truthfully to his neighbor, for we are all members of one body. ²⁶"In you anger do not sin": Do not let the sun go down while you are still angry, ²⁷and do not give the devil a foothold. ²⁸He who has been stealing must steal no longer, but must work, doing something useful with his own hands, that he may have something to share with those in need.
>
> ²⁹Do not let any unwholesome talk come out of your mouths, but only what is helpful for building others up according to their needs, that it may benefit those who listen. ³⁰And do not grieve the Holy Spirit of God, with whom you were sealed for the day of redemption. ³¹Get rid of all bitterness, rage and anger, brawling and slander, along with every form of malice. ³²Be kind and compassionate to one another, forgiving each other, just as in Christ God forgave you.

For example, verse 25 tells us to put off falsehood and speak the truth to our neighbors. Lying and truth-telling are contrasted. Find the other contrasts and list them below.

OLD SELF   NEW SELF

Which old-self practice do you have the most trouble putting to death?

70

Why is this one so difficult for you?

_____

_____

Which new-self practice do you do best?

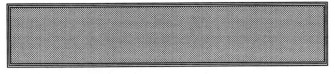

Why do you do so well at this one?

_____

_____

Would those around you say you are distinctive, that you are a "new self" person?

_____ Yes   _____ No

 PRAYER:
Thank God for truth you find in the last phrase of verse 32.

71

UNDILUTED LIVING

Be Pure

Purity may not be a topic that you leap around and do cartwheels over the opportunity to study. But you should.

To be pure is to see God (Matthew 5:8). The pure observe God everywhere, for He is everywhere. Others can't see Him, because they are impure. Life is ordinary, problems are hopeless, each day is a pressure cooker when you don't have purity in your surety that God is with you.

Do you want to see God in a daffodil? In a flat tire? In your child? In your daily routine? In your checkbook? Be pure, and you put on new glasses to see.

To be pure is to experience purity (wholeness and fullness) in your rewards. No person with mixed motives can experience the pure excitement of a singular purpose. No person with impure desires can enjoy pure contentment. No person with diluted dreams can feel the thrill of pure hope. No person with watered-down relationships can encounter pure intimacy, and its companion, pure joy.

Impurity dilutes the impact; it waters down the effect. A hundred pounds of pure TNT carries a far greater wallop than fifty pounds of TNT mixed with fifty pounds of straw.

Which would you rather have: Pure water or water with a touch of manure in it? 100% pure orange juice or juice with a little arsenic? Pure gasoline or gas with a bit of sludge? A pure gold necklace or one mixed with fool's gold? A pure bride or a girl tainted by just a few other men? A pure God or one with a pinch of unpredictable evil?

Which kind of follower does God desire to have: Pure or adulterated?

Which kind are you?

FOCUS:
Can you pray this and mean it? "Create in me a pure heart, O
God, and renew a steadfast spirit within me" (Psalm 51:10).

How to Desire a Pure Heart

How pure is your desire to be pure? Just how much do you really want
to be pure in thought (no lust), pure in business (no hedging), pure in
love (no self), pure in commitment (no laziness)? Circle one, or mark an
"X" in the vicinity.

| 100% | 80% | 55% | 45% | 30% | 5% |

Many Christians want to be pure, but not too pure, because they just
might miss out on some fun: an exciting R-rated movie, a bit of juicy gos-
sip, a sidesplitting but off-color joke, an enjoyable but self-serving
romance.

A key to developing a desire for a pure heart is found is Psalm 73.

> ¹**Surely God is good to Israel,**
>   **to those who are pure in heart.**
> ²**But as for me, my feet had almost slipped;**
>   **I had nearly lost my foothold.**
> ³**For I envied the arrogant**
>   **when I saw the prosperity of the wicked.**
> ⁴**They have no struggles;**
>   **their bodies are healthy and strong.**
> ⁵**They are free from the burdens common to man;**
>   **they are not plagued by human ills.**
> ⁶**Therefore pride is their necklace;**
>   **they clothe themselves with violence.**
> ⁷**From their callous hearts comes iniquity;**
>   **the evil conceits of their minds know no limits.**
> ⁸**They scoff, and speak with malice;**
>   **in their arrogance they threaten oppression.**
> ⁹**Their mouths lay claim to heaven,**
>   **and their tongues take possession of the earth.**
> ¹⁰**Therefore their people turn to them**
>   **and drink up waters in abundance.**

[11] They say, "How can God know?
   Does the Most High have knowledge?"

[12] This is what the wicked are like—
   always carefree, they increase in wealth.

[13] Surely in vain have I kept my heart pure;
   in vain have I washed my hands in innocence.

[14] All day long I have been plagued;
   I have been punished every morning.

[15] If I had said, "I will speak thus,"
   I would have betrayed your children.

[16] When I tried to understand all this,
   it was oppressive to me

[17] till I entered the sanctuary of God;
   then I understood their final destiny.

[18] Surely you place them on slippery ground;
   you cast them down to ruin.

[19] How suddenly are they destroyed,
   completely swept away by terrors!

[20] As a dream when one awakes,
   so when you arise, O Lord,
   you will despise them as fantasies.

[21] When my heart was grieved
   and my spirit embittered,

[22] I was senseless and ignorant;
   I was a brute beast before you.

[23] Yet I am always with you;
   you hold me by my right hand.

[24] You guide me with your counsel,
   and afterward you will take me into glory.

[25] Whom have I in heaven but you?
   And earth has nothing I desire besides you.

[26] My flesh and my heart may fail,
   but God is the strength of my heart
   and my portion forever.

[27] Those who are far from you will perish;
   you destroy all who are unfaithful to you.

[28] But as for me, it is good to be near God.
   I have made the Sovereign Lord my refuge;
   I will tell of all your deeds.

Answer these questions from the chapter.

1. What is the writer Asaph's belief in verse 1? _____

_____

2. Why do his feet almost slip? _____

_____

3. Why do you sometimes seek worldly things, long to do something you know is wrong, stray from purity? What tempts you to slip up?

_____

_____

_____

_____

4. What beliefs in Asaph's prayer restored his desire for purity of relationship with God?

```
┌─────────────────────────────────────────────────────┐
│                                                     │
│                                                     │
│                                                     │
└─────────────────────────────────────────────────────┘
```

PRAYER:
Examine your true beliefs with God.
Do you believe verse 1?
Do you trust the statements you wrote in Question 4?

TUESDAY

FOCUS:
Turn back to Psalm 73 and pray aloud verses 23-28.

How easy or hard was it to pray those words and mean them?

Easy ◄————————————————————► Hard

(If it wasn't especially easy, try praying them again, slowly.)

How to Desire a Pure Heart: II

If you could choose to see ONLY ONE of these sights, which one would you choose?

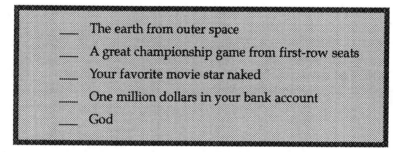

Here are some passages that describe someone seeing God. What is it like to see Him? Take notes below from Isaiah 6:1-4; Ezekiel 1:25-28; and Revelation 1:12-18.

¹**In the year that King Uzziah died, I saw the Lord seated on a throne, high and exalted, and the train of his robe filled the temple. ²Above him were seraphs, each with six wings: With two wings they covered their faces, with two they covered their feet, and with two they were flying. ³And they were calling to one another:**

**"Holy, holy, holy is the Lᴏʀᴅ Almighty;
the whole earth is full of his glory."**

⁴**At the sound of their voices the doorposts and thresholds shook and the temple was filled with smoke.**

[25]Then there came a voice from above the expanse over their heads as they stood with lowered wings. [26]Above the expanse over their heads was what looked like a throne of sapphire, and high above on the throne was a figure like that of a man. [27]I saw that from what appeared to be his waist up he looked like glowing metal, as if full of fire, and that from there down he looked like fire; and brilliant light surrounded him. [28]Like the appearance of a rainbow in the clouds on a rainy day, so was the radiance around him.

[12]I turned around to see the voice that was speaking to me. And when I turned I saw seven golden lampstands, [13]and among the lampstands was someone "like a son of man," dressed in a robe reaching down to his feet and with a golden sash around his chest. [14]His head and hair were white like wool, as white as snow, and his eyes were like blazing fire. [15]His feet were like bronze glowing in a furnace, and his voice was like the sound of rushing waters. [16]In his right hand he held seven stars, and out of his mouth came a sharp double-edged sword. His face was like the sun shining in all its brilliance.

[17]When I saw him, I fell at his feet as though dead. Then he placed his right hand on me and said: "Do not be afraid. I am the First and the Last. [18]I am the Living One; I was dead, and behold I am alive for ever and ever! And I hold the keys of death and Hades."

Do you want to see God?　　____ Yes　　____ No

Why would you want to see God?

_____

_____

Is there any reason you would be hesitant to see God?

_____

_____

The pure in heart WILL see God. What will happen when they do? Circle it.

[1]How great is the love the Father has lavished on us, that we should be called children of God! And that is what we are! The reason the world does not know us is that it did not know him. [2]Dear friends, now we are children of God, and what we will be has not yet been made known. But we know that when he appears, we shall be like him, for we shall see him as he is (1 John 3:1-2).

If you believed this promise, what would you do? Verse 3 tells you:
Everyone who has this hope in him purifies himself, just as he is pure.

_____

_____

PRAYER:
Ask God, "King of Glory, what impurity in me is keeping me from seeing you more clearly now or in the future?"

WEDNESDAY

FOCUS:
Confess any impurities from yesterday; don't just confess,
but grieve over the harm they did to you, Jesus and others.

Where in Me Does God Want Purity?

Maybe a better question is, "Where does God NOT want purity?" Put a star
(✳) by those areas in which God doesn't care about how pure you are.

language	_____	speech, promises,
tasies, dreams	_____	thought life, fan-
giving	_____	love, generosity,
	_____	finances, business,

Where do you most need purity at this time in your life? Check (✓) one
of the above cases.

Is a little bit of impurity all right with God, excusable since we are "only
human"? Is it okay to have just one area of enjoyable sin, as long as the rest
of your life is pretty clean? What lesson do you learn from Acts 5:1-11?

¹Now a man named Ananias, together with his wife Sapphira, also sold a
piece of property. ²With his wife's full knowledge he kept back part of the
money for himself, but brought the rest and put it at the apostles' feet.

³Then Peter said, "Ananias, how is it that Satan has so filled your heart
that you have lied to the Holy Spirit and have kept for yourself some of the
money you received for the land? ⁴Didn't it belong to you before it was sold?
And after it was sold, wasn't the money at your disposal? What made you
think of doing such a thing? You have not lied to men but to God."

⁵When Ananias heard this, he fell down and died. And great fear seized all
who heard what had happened. ⁶Then the young men came forward, wrapped
up his body, and carried him out and buried him.

⁷About three hours later his wife came in, not knowing what had happened. ⁸Peter asked her, "Tell me, is this the price you and Ananias got for
the land?"

"Yes," she said, "that is the price."

Peter said to her, "How could you agree to test the Spirit of the Lord? Look! The feet of the men who buried your husband are at the door, and they will carry you out also."

At that moment she fell down at his feet and died. Then the young men came in and, finding her dead, carried her out and buried her beside her husband. Great fear seized the whole church and all who heard about these events.

Often, Christians have a pet sin, something they know is wrong, but rationalize as not so bad. What impurity are you most likely to excuse or brush off as not serious, wrong but acceptable?

To rationalize is simply to tell yourself "rational – lies." These lies or excuses sound good until put under cross-examination.

Imagine yourself confessing this "small sin" to your spouse, to your mom, to your pastor. Does the size of the "small sin" suddenly magnify when you think of telling it out loud?

PRAYER:
Pray over James 4:4-10.

You adulterous people, don't you know that friendship with the world is hatred toward God? Anyone who chooses to be a friend of the world becomes an enemy of God. Or do you think Scripture says without reason that the spirit he caused to live in us envies intensely? But he gives us more grace. That is why Scripture says:

"God opposes the proud
but gives grace to the humble."

Submit yourselves, then, to God. Resist the devil, and he will flee from you. Come near to God and he will come near to you. Wash your hands, you sinners, and purify your hearts, you double-minded. Grieve, mourn and wail. Change your laughter to mourning and your joy to gloom. Humble yourselves before the Lord, and he will lift you up.

THURSDAY

FOCUS:
See God again . . . and open your heart to let Him see you.

How Can One Gain a Pure Heart?

Imagine your family is going to an important wedding. You must get your six-year-old son ready to leave in 45 minutes because he is the ring-bearer. You look out in the backyard and you don't see your son, you see Pigpen from the Peanuts comic strip! He's a filthy mess. What will you do to get him cleaned up and keep him clean until the ceremony?

☞ _____   ☞ _____

☞ _____   ☞ _____

☞ _____   ☞ _____

What parallels do you see in this story and the establishment and maintenance of your purity?

☞ _____   ☞ _____

☞ _____   ☞ _____

☞ _____   ☞ _____

Which step do you need to take to improve your purity?

____ Admit you are dirty. (Your eight-year-old may say, "But, Mom, I'm clean!") Proverbs 20:9 asserts,

"Who can say, 'I have kept my heart pure; I am clean and without sin'?"

____ Allow yourself to be washed in pure water. (He may say, "I'll wash later. Do I have to use soap?") First Corinthians 6:9-11 states,

[9]Do you not know that the wicked will not inherit the kingdom of God? Do not be deceived: Neither the sexually immoral nor idolaters nor adulterers nor male prostitutes nor homosexual offenders [10]nor thieves nor the greedy nor drunkards nor slanderers nor swindlers will inherit the kingdom of God. [11]And that is what some of you were. But you were washed, you were sanctified, you were justified in the name of the Lord Jesus Christ and by the Spirit of our God.

___ Avoid the actions and places you generally get dirty. (You tell your son, "Don't go back outside!") Proverbs 4:14-15 commands,

> **14Do not set foot on the path of the wicked**
> **or walk in the way of evil men.**
> **15Avoid it, do not travel on it;**
> **turn from it and go on your way.**

___ Seek a clean alternative. (You can't expect a six-year-old child to simply sit still, so you focus him on a coloring book or a video.) Philippians 4:8-9 suggests:

> **8Finally, brothers, whatever is true, whatever is noble, whatever is right, whatever is pure, whatever is lovely, whatever is admirable—if anything is excellent or praiseworthy—think about such things. 9Whatever you have learned or received or heard from me, or seen in me— put it into practice. And the God of peace will be with you.**

___ Be vigilant. (The six-year-old in us will seek to go back to the mud.) Hebrews 10:23-25 declares,

> **23Let us hold unswervingly to the hope we profess, for he who promised is faithful. 24And let us consider how we may spur one another on toward love and good deeds. 25Let us not give up meeting together, as some are in the habit of doing, but let us encourage one another—and all the more as you see the Day approaching.**

 PRAYER:
Like anything precious, purity has a price. Are you willing to pay it?

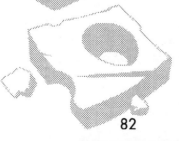

FRIDAY

FOCUS:
Lord, what did I do right in protecting my purity yesterday? Where did I let You down?

How Can I Be Pure without Being Prudish?

Some Christians don't want to become too pure because they don't want to become legalistic, artificial, holier-than-thou, stiff, or boring. But there is a big difference between being pure and being puritanical. Write down what you think is the meaning of each of these liberating, exciting passages (you may be surprised!).

Titus 2:15:
> **These, then, are the things you should teach. Encourage and rebuke with all authority. Do not let anyone despise you.**

_____

_____

Colossians 2:20-23:
> **²⁰Since you died with Christ to the basic principles of this world, why, as though you still belonged to it, do you submit to its rules: ²¹"Do not handle! Do not taste! Do not touch!"? ²²These are all destined to perish with use, because they are based on human commands and teachings. ²³Such regulations indeed have an appearance of wisdom, with their self-imposed worship, their false humility and their harsh treatment of the body, but they lack any value in restraining sensual indulgence.**

_____

_____

Mark 7:1-23:
> **¹The Pharisees and some of the teachers of the law who had come from Jerusalem gathered around Jesus and ²saw some of his disciples eating food with hands that were "unclean," that is, unwashed. ³(The Pharisees and all the Jews do not eat unless they give their hands a ceremonial washing, holding to the tradition of the elders. ⁴When they come from the marketplace they do not eat unless they wash. And they observe many other traditions, such as the washing of cups, pitchers and kettles.)**
> **⁵So the Pharisees and teachers of the law asked Jesus, "Why don't your**

disciples live according to the tradition of the elders instead of eating their food with 'unclean' hands?"

⁶He replied, "Isaiah was right when he prophesied about you hypocrites; as it is written:

> "'These people honor me with their lips,
>   but their hearts are far from me.
> ⁷They worship me in vain;
>   their teachings are but rules taught by men.'

⁸You have let go of the commands of God and are holding on to the traditions of men."

⁹And he said to them: "You have a fine way of setting aside the commands of God in order to observe your own traditions! For Moses said, ¹⁰'Honor your father and your mother,' and, 'Anyone who curses his father or mother must be put to death.' ¹¹But you say that if a man says to his father or mother: 'Whatever help you might otherwise have received from me is Corban' (that is, a gift devoted to God), ¹²then you no longer let him do anything for his father or mother. ¹³Thus, you nullify the word of God by your tradition that you have handed down. And you do many things like that."

¹⁴Again Jesus called the crowd to him and said, "Listen to me, everyone, and understand this. ¹⁵Nothing outside a man can make him 'unclean' by going into him. Rather, it is what comes out of a man that makes him 'unclean.'"

¹⁷After he had left the crowd and entered the house, his disciples asked him about this parable. ¹⁸"Are you so dull?" he asked. "Don't you see that nothing that enters a man from the outside can make him 'unclean'? ¹⁹For it doesn't go into his heart but into his stomach, and then out of his body." (In saying this, Jesus declared all foods "clean.")

²⁰He went on: "What comes out of a man is what makes him 'unclean.' ²¹For from within, out of men's hearts, come evil thoughts, sexual immorality, theft, murder, adultery, ²²greed, malice, deceit, lewdness, envy, slander, arrogance and folly. ²³All these evils come from inside and make a man 'unclean.'"

PRUDISHNESS is fear-based. It avoids doing anything that will make it feel guilty or make God mad.

PURITY is love-based. It wants to see God, honor God, bless God.

PRUDISHNESS is self-centered. It hopes to escape hell and enter heaven.

PURITY is other-centered. It hopes to lead others out of hell and into heaven.

PRUDISHNESS is rules-centered. It does exactly what the rule says, no matter what the reasons or the effect on people.

PURITY is reason-centered. It thinks through and prays about the effect of any action.

PRUDISHNESS condemns the world and tries to escape it.

PURITY hurts for the world and tries to transform it.

PRUDISHNESS focuses on avoiding evil and is suspicious of fun.

PURITY focuses on God's good gifts and can't help but have a good time.

 PRAYER:
Lord, remind me when my actions are prudish and self-righteous. Give me a heart that longs for purity and holiness in all my thoughts and actions.

PLAY IT SMART
Living Life with Wisdom

M ark each statement with either "A" for agree for "D" for disagree.

_____ Most people think they are pretty smart.

_____ Most people do things that ruin their chances to have the very things they most want.

_____ Most people get themselves into the vast majority of the messes in which they end up.

_____ Most people think that their problems are not their own fault, but others are to blame.

_____ Most people are not especially content, satisfied, or happy.

_____ Most people make the same mistake more than once.

_____ Most people make at least one mistake over and over and over until it becomes so painful they must stop or it kills them.

_____ Most of what people do to make themselves feel better ends up making them feel worse.

_____ Most people who think they are smart are not as smart as they think.

We live in the most educated era in history. There are more preschools, elementary schools, private schools, graduate schools and night schools than ever before. We have bookstores, informative publications, educational programs by the armload. More people obtain Ph.D.s, attend seminars and go "online" than at any previous time.

But **"although they claimed to be wise, they became fools"** (Romans 1:22). It seems the smarter we get, the more ways we find to make fools of ourselves.

"Where is the wise man? Where is the scholar? Where is the philosopher of this age? Has not God made foolish the wisdom of the world?" (1 Corinthians 1:20).

Get smart!

FOCUS:
Ask God to show you what He wants you to pray about!

Read our whole passage for the week, Ephesians 5:13-21, and write a one-sentence summary.

¹³But everything exposed by the light becomes visible, ¹⁴for it is light that makes everything visible. This is why it is said:

"Wake up, O sleeper,
    rise from the dead,
and Christ will shine on you."

¹⁵Be very careful, then, how you live—not as unwise but as wise, ¹⁶making the most of every opportunity, because the days are evil. ¹⁷Therefore do not be foolish, but understand what the Lord's will is. ¹⁸Do not get drunk on wine, which leads to debauchery. Instead, be filled with the Spirit. ¹⁹Speak to one another with psalms, hymns and spiritual songs. Sing and make music in your heart to the Lord, ²⁰always giving thanks to God the Father for everything, in the name of our Lord Jesus Christ.

²¹Submit to one another out of reverence for Christ.

The Bible often contrasts light and darkness. What does the light do according to verse 13?

Have you done anything in the past few days that, if others knew, would embarrass you?

___ cursing	___ gossiping
___ woman watching	___ man watching
___ spending money selfishly	___ blowing up at the kids
___ hedging the truth	___ your choice _____

If the apostle Paul shadowed you for a week, what would you probably do differently? Work harder? Pray more? Carry your Bible? Do more good deeds? What?

1. _____

2. _____

3. _____

Who *does* shadow you everyday? Read Ephesians 1:13-14.

¹³And you also were included in Christ when you heard the word of truth, the gospel of your salvation. Having believed, you were marked in him with a seal, the promised Holy Spirit, ¹⁴who is a deposit guaranteeing our inheritance until the redemption of those who are God's possession—to the praise of his glory.

The light is not just shined on you, the Light is *in* you and *with* you. What one area of your life will you make more lightworthy?

_____

PRAYER:
Shine a light on Jesus in your prayer by praising Him for His flawless quality.

TUESDAY

FOCUS:
What is weighing on your heart today?

Figure up how many days you have lived and how many days you have to go (hopefully):

Years lived so far: _____

$\times$ 365

Total days lived: [ ]

Age minus 75 = _____

$\times$ 365

Total days to go: [ ]

Mark an "X" at the point you think (hope) you are on the time line.

| -- |
Birth   Death

How do you feel about where you are on your life progression?

_____

_____

_____

How well have you lived Ephesians 5:15-16? **Be very careful, then, how you live—not as unwise but as wise, making the most of every opportunity, because the days are evil.**

____ A = Outstanding   ____ B = Above average

____ C = About average   ____ D = below average

____ F = Failing

89

What has been the worst waste of time in your life so far?

_____

_____

_____

_____

_____

What has been the best use of your time so far?

_____

_____

_____

_____

_____

How could Jesus answer the last two questions in regard to you?

Worst _____

_____

_____

Best _____

_____

_____

PRAYER:
Pray about one way you could make the most of your time for the next few days.

WEDNESDAY

FOCUS:
Evaluate your use of the 1,440 minutes the Lord gave you yesterday.

In Ephesians 5:17, what is the opposite of understanding the Lord's will? **Therefore, do not be foolish, but understand what the Lord's will is.**

```
┌─────────────────────────────────────────────┐
│                                             │
│                                             │
└─────────────────────────────────────────────┘
```

Do you really believe anything outside of God's plan is silly, stupid, and dumb?

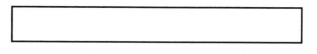

_____ Yes   _____ No

What does it say we should and shouldn't be filled with in verse 18? **Do not get drunk on wine, which leads to debauchery. Instead, be filled with the Spirit.**

Should not _____

Should _____

Alcohol is an artificial stimulant and depressant. Many people see drinking as a stress reliever, an escape mechanism, or even a confidence builder. But liquor is not the only method of artificial stimulation/relaxation. List some other things people drink, eat, inject, or do to cope with pressure.

_____   _____

_____   _____

_____   _____

Let's say you have had a long, hard, tiring, stress-filled day of work, problems, deadlines, children, phone calls, and decisions. You are worn out, and it is only Monday. It is 9:30 p.m. What would you normally do to unwind and forget it all?

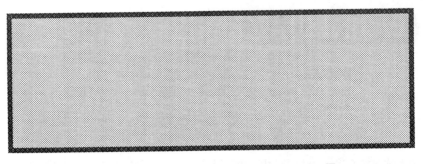

Does this method usually work well?　　❏　Yes　　　　❏　No

Has God said He would fill you with His Spirit and power through this
activity?　　　　　　　　　　　　　❏　Yes　　　　❏　No

 PRAYER:
Pray about your use of anything worldly or artificial to fill
you.

FOCUS:
What did you do to rejuvenate yourself yesterday? Pray about it.

Ephesians 5:18-21 is actually one long sentence in the original Greek. It literally reads, **"Be filled with the Holy Spirit by speaking to one another with psalms . . . by singing and making music in your heart . . . by giving thanks to God . . . and by submitting to one another."**

The Lord has not said He would refill us through watching Monday night football, eating chocolate chip ice cream, or taking a hot bubble bath. He might use these methods to help you chill out, but He has not guaranteed their results. God has promised to spark us spiritually through praise, thankfulness, prayer, and humility.

What do you generally focus on or occupy your mind with during these parts of your day? (Be specific. If it's radio, name what station and type of music; if it's silent thoughts, what kind of thoughts?)

First thing in the morning _____

Driving to work _____

At lunch or breaks _____

Driving home _____

Making dinner _____

Free evenings _____

Just before bed _____

Would you refill your engine crankcase with dirty oil? Would you pick food up off the bathroom floor and eat it? Would you put rat poison on your child's sandwich?

Don't be suckered into the world's philosophy that a little trashy music or a little raunchy TV is to be expected and accepted. Protect yourself and the young minds in your home from the sludge of society. Be filled with God's pure Spirit instead.

PRAYER:
Father, where do You want me to insert praise, prayer, and thanksgiving into my day?

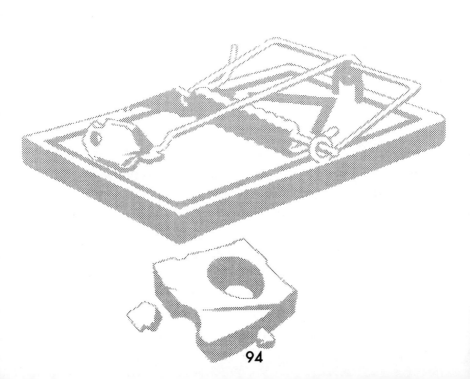

94

FOCUS:
Did I do the "same ol' same ol'" yesterday or refill with God's Spirit?

How would you define these words:

Always: _____

_____

Everything: _____

_____

Thanksgiving: _____

_____

Now put Ephesians 5:20 in your own words. **Always giving thanks to God the Father for everything, in the name of our Lord Jesus Christ.**

_____

_____

_____

Which do you generally do more: complain or give thanks? Wish things were different or appreciate the things you have? Shade in each "out box" to the degree you gripe or rejoice.

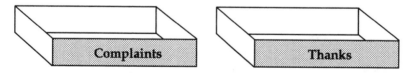

List some things about which you usually complain and some things for which you commonly give thanks.

COMPLAINTS	THANKS

PRAYER:
Prayerfully consider how complaining and thanksgiving affect you. List these common effects in the appropriate column.

COMPLAINTS	THANKS

Ask God for His view of each attitude.

LIVING ABOVE THE RULES
Respect Authority

Are you a rebel or a conformist? Always putting a toe over the line or staying back at least five feet from it, just to be safe? Resisting authority or respecting it?

Romans 13:1-2 carries an uncomfortable and hardly American mandate: **[1]"Everyone must submit himself to the governing authorities, for there is no authority except that which God has established. The authorities that exist have been established by God. [2]Consequently, he who rebels against the authority is rebelling against what God has instituted, and those who do so will bring judgment on themselves."**

Authorities include the government, family, and employment arenas.

Daniel submitted to and served the pagan king, Nebuchadnezzar. David would not take part in a coup against the demon-possessed King Saul. Jesus submitted to parents who were his inferiors.

Unless God's commands were being abrogated, Bible heroes obeyed the authorities over them. But respecting authority does not mean you endorse its every move. You respect out of respect for God. The only good reason to rebel is a godly reason.

If you are a rebel, do you fight for Christ or for self?

If you are in authority, you must respect the authority you have been given by not abusing it. Do you use your power to get your way or glorify God's way? Do you rely on artificial power of your title (president, foreman, father, mother) or on true authority of character? Whenever you resort to the artificial power of your position, you forfeit some of that power. Authority is like money in the bank: the less you use, the more interest it accrues.

MONDAY

FOCUS:
Lord, I am not the authority. You are the authority. I will
obey what You teach me this week.

Read Ephesians 6:1-9 and jot below your immediate, gut reaction to what
you read.

¹Children, obey your parents in the Lord, for this is right. ²"Honor your
father and mother"—which is the first commandment with a promise—
³"that it may go well with you and that you may enjoy long life on the earth."

⁴Fathers, do not exasperate your children; instead, bring them up in the
training and instruction of the Lord.

⁵Slaves, obey your earthly masters with respect and fear, and with sin-
cerity of heart, just as you would obey Christ. ⁶Obey them not only to win their
favor when their eye is on you, but like slaves of Christ, doing the will of God
from your heart. ⁷Serve wholeheartedly, as if you were serving the Lord, not
men, ⁸because you know that the Lord will reward everyone for whatever
good he does, whether he is slave or free.

⁹And masters, treat your slaves in the same way. Do not threaten them,
since you know that he who is both their Master and yours is in heaven, and
there is no favoritism with him.

_____

_____

_____

_____

Paul gives comments to four categories of people: children, fathers, slaves
and masters. With what motivation or reasoning does He give His commands to them?

Children: _____

_____

Fathers: _____

_____

Slaves: _____

_____

Did you notice that the motivation for the commands is not just a "what" but a "who"? Fill in each blank.

verse 1: "Obey your parents ____ _____ _____ ."

verse 4: "the training and instruction ____ _____ _____ ."

verse 7: "Serve...as if serving _____ _____ , not _____ ."

verse 9: "Do not threaten them, since . . . he who is both their _____

and yours is in _____ , _____ _____ ____ _____

_____ _____ _____ ."

We respect and obey authority, not because parents or bosses are perfect, but because we respect God. We treat children or employees with consideration not because they measure up, but because the Lord gives consideration to us. Don't fall into the trap of basing your respect level on the other person's respectability level. If you do, you will always be a judge, never a servant; always a critic, never a guide.

 PRAYER:
Declare your respect for God's total authority.

TUESDAY

FOCUS:
Can you praise God for being your Father?

What three words would you use to describe your dad?

1. _____

2. _____

3. _____

Your mom?

1. _____

2. _____

3. _____

What two things are children told to do in regard to their parents?

Ephesians 6:1   1. _____

Ephesians 6:2   2. _____

Define each word in your own words:

1. _____

2. _____

Two qualifiers: First, children must comply, but only "in the Lord." Should a parent command an action outside of God's will, a child may resist. **"We must obey God rather than men"** (Acts 5:29). Second, it seems that children are to obey parents until they "leave father and mother" and are united as husband and wife (Acts 5:31). They no longer need to obey, but should continue to honor mom and dad (and not merely on Mother's Day or Father's Day). What have you done to honor your parents lately?

- _____   • _____

- _____   • _____

What one thing could you do in the next week that would really shower them with honor?

☆ _____

What if parents are dishonorable, unkind, abusive, alcoholic? You still must give them honor, but no longer have to "obey" them by accepting their criticism or allowing their views to run your life.

What if parents are dead? Honor them by speaking well of them to their grandchildren.

 PRAYER:
Forgive your parents and pledge to honor them. Accept the promise in Ephesians 6:3.

FOCUS:
Pray for your parents and your children.

If you have children, what rules would *they* say are the most important ones you have taught them?

❑ Look your best   ❑ Go to church

❑ Be on time   ❑ Love others

❑ Save your money   ❑ Be forgiving

❑ Serve the Lord   ❑ Be generous

❑ Eat your vegetables   ❑ If you can't say something nice . . .

❑ Graduate from college ❑ Other _____

More lessons are caught than taught. By watching you, what would they say is most important in life?

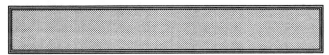

Fathers, how well have you followed Ephesians 6:4?

POOR -- PERFECT

Exasperating children results from giving them arbitrary, unexplained or unloving rules. Which of each are you?

   ___   explaining / unexplaining   ___

   ___   discussing / arbitrary   ___

   ___   loving / unloving   ___

As one charged with raising kids in the training of the Lord, what would you say your children have learned about the Lord directly from you (not from church, Sunday School, etc.)?

_____   _____

_____   _____

PRAYER:

Prayerfully decide what you believe would be God's top three goals for your children.

1. _____

2. _____

3. _____

Name one thing you could do to instruct or lead them in reaching each goal.

1. _____

2. _____

3. _____

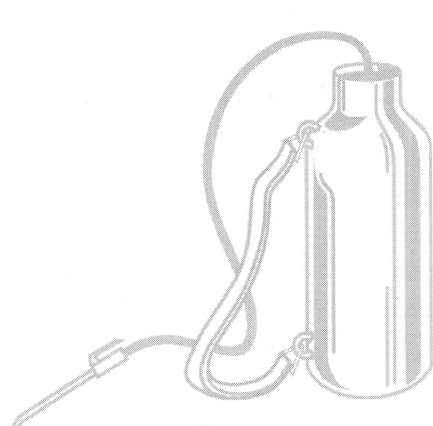

THURSDAY

FOCUS:
What did (or didn't) you teach your kids about the Lord yesterday?

For what do you do the job/work you do?

___	money	___	challenge
___	family	___	the Lord
___	the good	___	survival

What is your job-contentment rating?

| --- |

Love it!   Hate it!

In spite of the fact that you are not a slave (though you may feel like it), what principles do you find for yourself in Ephesians 6:5-8?

> ⁵Slaves, obey your earthly masters with respect and fear, and with sincerity of heart, just as you would obey Christ. ⁶Obey them not only to win their favor when their eye is on you, but like slaves of Christ, doing the will of God from your heart. ⁷Serve wholeheartedly, as if you were serving the Lord, not men, ⁸because you know that the Lord will reward everyone for whatever good he does, whether he is slave or free.

According to Paul, what should your attitude be toward your boss/superior if he/she is capable, caring, and considerate?

What should your attitude be if he/she is incompetent, apathetic and unkind?

Name one thing that would change about you or your job if you had these attitudes?

```

```

When was the last time you witnessed on the job? In the past . . .

a) day   b) week   c) month   d) year   e) never

Actually, you witnessed on the job the last time you went to work. Your effort and attitude is a witness as a Christian, either glorifying Christ or besmirching His name.

 PRAYER:
Read today's verses again prayerfully.

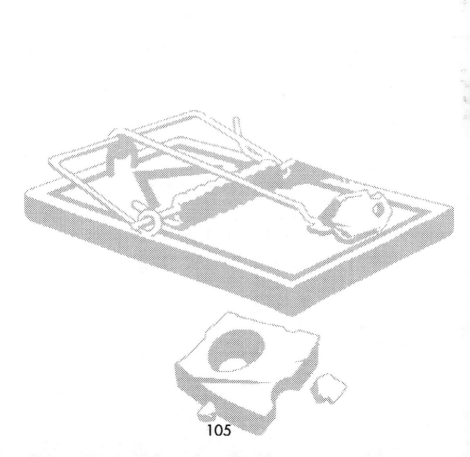

FRIDAY

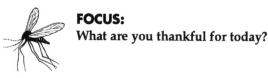

FOCUS:
What are you thankful for today?

☐ Agree   ☐ Disagree   "Good help is hard to find."

How do you want to be treated by your employer/supervisor? Name four things you want.

1. _____
2. _____
3. _____
4. _____

List the people you supervise on the job or pay in any way (Example: secretary, waitress, kid who mows the yard).

____ _____   ____ _____

____ _____   ____ _____

Find four things you are told to do in Ephesians 6:9 and Colossians 4:1?

And masters, treat your slaves in the same way. Do not threaten them, since you know that he who is both their Master and yours is in heaven, and there is no favoritism with him.

Masters, provide your slaves with what is right and fair, because you know that you also have a Master in heaven.

1. _____   3. _____
2. _____   4. _____

What kind of a "Master" has God been to you? Describe His . . .

Compensation _____

_____

Patience _____

_____

Helpfulness _____

_____

Encouragement _____

_____

How do you think each of the people you listed above would rate you as a supervisor? Put a "G" by their name if they would say you are a 'godly' overseer; an "S" if you are more a slavemaster; and, an "N" if you are neutral.

PRAYER:
Use John 13:1-17 as a basis for praising God.

¹It was just before the Passover Feast. Jesus knew that the time had come for him to leave this world and go to the Father. Having loved his own who were in the world, he now showed them the full extent of his love.

²The evening meal was being served, and the devil had already prompted Judas Iscariot, son of Simon, to betray Jesus. ³Jesus knew that the Father had put all things under his power, and that he had come from God and was returning to God; ⁴so he got up from the meal, took off his outer clothing, and wrapped a towel around his waist. ⁵After that, he poured water into a basin and began to wash his disciples' feet, drying them with the towel that was wrapped around him.

⁶He came to Simon Peter, who said to him, "Lord, are you going to wash my feet?"

⁷Jesus replied, "You do not realize now what I am doing, but later you will understand."

⁸"No," said Peter, "you shall never wash my feet."

Jesus answered, "Unless I wash you, you have no part with me."

⁹"Then, Lord," Simon Peter replied, "not just my feet but my hands and my head as well!"

¹⁰Jesus answered, "A person who has had a bath needs only to wash his feet; his whole body is clean. And you are clean, though not every one of you." ¹¹For he knew who was going to betray him, and that was why he said not every one was clean.

¹²When he had finished washing their feet, he put on his clothes and returned to his place. "Do you understand what I have done for you?" he asked them. ¹³"You call me 'Teacher' and 'Lord,' and rightly so, for that is what I am. ¹⁴Now that I, your Lord and Teacher, have washed your feet, you also should wash one another's feet. ¹⁵I have set you an example that you

should do as I have done for you. [16]I tell you the truth, no servant is greater than his master, nor is a messenger greater than the one who sent him. [17]Now that you know these things, you will be blessed if you do them.

NO SLEEPING ON THE JOB

Stay Alert

H ere are some words you never want to have to say or hear:

> "If only you had noticed the warning signs sooner. Now the cancer has spread too far."
>
> "Officer, I only dozed off for a moment! It all happened so fast."
>
> "How could we have been so blind? Our son has been doing drugs all this time!"
>
> "I was asleep at the switch, boss. I missed the big deal."
>
> "I just wasn't paying attention. I thought we were happily married."
>
> "I should have seen it coming. He was desperate. I just didn't know he would take his own life."

Accidents. Missed opportunities. Lost relationships. All because we don't stay alert.

Jesus repeated so often, "He who has ears to hear, let him hear."

But most people did not have hearing ears, ears pricked to the whisper of God's voice. Most did not recognize Jesus as the expected Messiah. Even John the Baptist asked, **"Are you the one who is to come or should we expect another?"** Jesus answered John's messengers, **"Go back and report to John what you hear and see: The blind receive sight, the lame walk, . . . the deaf hear, the dead are raised, and the good news is preached to the poor. Blessed is the man who does not fall away on account of me."**

In other words, Jesus is saying, "It is obvious what's happening and who I am, to anyone who is alert."

Jesus also said, "I am with you always." Are you awake to His presence today? Do you have ears to hear Him? Eyes to see Him? Knowledge of the Word to discern truth?

Don't be spiritually nearsighted. Be alert to God's work in and around you today.

FOCUS:
Give thanks to the LORD for he is good.
His love endures forever (Psalm 136:1).

If you had to go one-on-one in a battle of wits, brute strength and determination against one of the following people, who would you choose?

◊ Arnold Schwarzenegger

◊ O.J. Simpson's lawyers

◊ Satan

◊ Barney Fife

Who would you *least* want to battle? _____

Which one are you battling regularly already? _____

What would you say is the main message of Ephesians 6:10-20?

> [10]**Finally, be strong in the Lord and in his mighty power.** [11]**Put on the full armor of God so that you can take your stand against the devil's schemes.** [12]**For our struggle is not against flesh and blood, but against the rulers, against the authorities, against the powers of this dark world and against the spiritual forces of evil in the heavenly realms.** [13]**Therefore put on the full armor of God, so that when the day of evil comes, you may be able to stand your ground, and after you have done everything, to stand.** [14]**Stand firm then, with the belt of truth buckled around your waist, with the breastplate of righteousness in place,** [15]**and with your feet fitted with the readiness that comes from the gospel of peace.** [16]**In addition to all this, take up the shield of faith, with which you can extinguish all the flaming arrows of the evil one.** [17]**Take the helmet of salvation and the sword of the Spirit, which is the word of God.** [18]**And pray in the Spirit on all occasions with all kinds of prayers and requests. With this in mind, be alert and always keep on praying for all the saints.**
>
> [19]**Pray also for me, that whenever I open my mouth, words may be given me so that I will fearlessly make known the mystery of the gospel,** [20]**for which I am an ambassador in chains. Pray that I may declare it fearlessly, as I should.**

*Main
Message*

Verse 10 says:

"Be strong in the _____ and in _____."

Whose power do you tend to rely upon most days?

     ___ the Lord's   ___ your own

Notice Paul says twice that we are to put on God's *full armor*. The helmet isn't much good if the arrow strikes your chest. Partial armor is not enough. Where your armor is strongest, mark an "S"; where it is weakest, mark a "W."

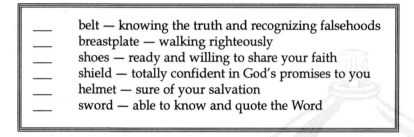

___	belt — knowing the truth and recognizing falsehoods
___	breastplate — walking righteously
___	shoes — ready and willing to share your faith
___	shield — totally confident in God's promises to you
___	helmet — sure of your salvation
___	sword — able to know and quote the Word

PRAYER:
Ask God what armor He most wants you to put on today.

TUESDAY

FOCUS:
Though I walk in the midst of trouble,
    you preserve my life;
you stretch out your hand against the anger of my foes,
    with your right hand you save me (Psalm 138:7).

Who are your foes, according to Ephesians 6:12? **For our struggle is not against flesh and blood, but against the rulers, against the authorities, against the powers of this dark world and against the spiritual forces of evil in the heavenly realms.**

✠ _____   ✠ _____

✠ _____   ✠ _____

How do you feel, knowing who and what you are up against? Like a . . .

> ___ tiger, ready to fight
> ___ chicken, ready for flight
> ___ turtle, ready to hide
> ___ hyena, ready to laugh

How would you define the word "scheme"?

_____

_____

The devil has schemes for you, verse 11 tells us. How gullible are you? How susceptible are you to tricks and illusions? Mark an "X."

| -- |
gullible   alert

The tempter is most likely to trip you up the same way he has time and time again in the past. Like Lucy holding a football in front of Charlie Brown, Satan holds out some "football" to you, over and over, and you keep falling for it? What is it?

___ sexual desire	___ juicy gossip
___ workaholism	___ escapism through TV
___ angry outbursts	___ "I can do it myself" attitude

___ what? _____

PRAYER:
Why are you a target in this area? Do you know? Ask God to show you your weakness and His remedy for it. Write the thoughts He gives you below:

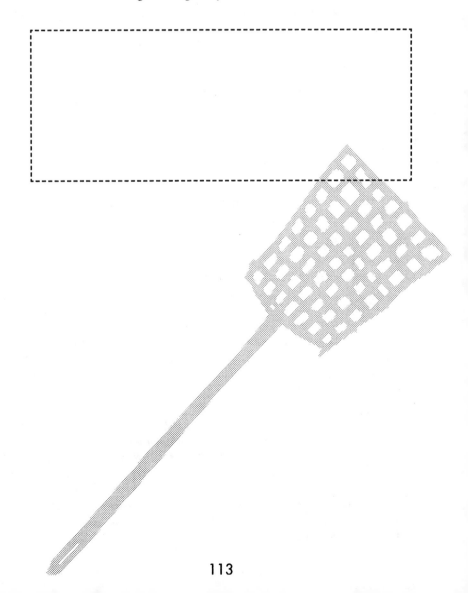

WEDNESDAY

FOCUS:
You make me glad by your deeds, O LORD;
I sing for joy at the works of your hands (Psalm 92:4).

Read Ephesians 6:13. **Therefore, put on the full armor of God, so that when the day of evil comes, you may be able to stand your ground, and after you have done everything, to stand.**

Describe one of the really bad times in your life and what made it so bad.

_____

_____

_____

_____

What sustained you during that evil time?

_____

_____

_____

Are you ready for another "evil day" or hard time?

___ Yes	___ No	___ Unsure

If your answer is not "yes," you may be in trouble! More evil times are sure to come. The death of a parent, the rebellion of a son, the divorce of a daughter, a downturn in the economy, a war, the loss of health with increasing age. You will not go unscathed. What is God's primary goal for you when you face an ordeal? The word is used four times in verses 11-14.

¹¹Put on the full armor of God so that you can take your stand against the devil's schemes. ¹²For our struggle is not against flesh and blood, but against the rulers, against the authorities, against the powers of this dark world and against the spiritual forces of evil in the heavenly realms. ¹³Therefore put on the full armor of God, so that when the day of evil comes, you may be able to stand your ground, and after you have done everything, to stand. ¹⁴Stand firm then, with the belt of truth buckled around your waist, with the breastplate of righteousness in place . . . .

The word is:

The boxer left standing at the end of a knockout fight may not look pretty, but he is the winner. He may have been knocked down or even out of the ring, but he didn't stay down or out.

Your goal as a Christian going through a crisis is to finish standing up. You may, during the difficult, dark rounds, go down, get hit, cry out, or backtrack, as long as you never throw in the towel.

 PRAYER:
Father, am I ready for the evil day, the valley of the shadow, the flood?

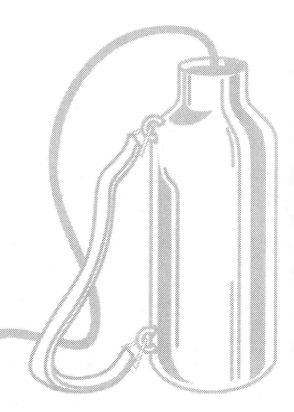

THURSDAY

FOCUS:
Even though I walk
        through the valley of the shadow of death,
I will fear no evil,
        for you are with me (Psalm 23:4).

Let's focus on the believer's shield for the rest of today's lesson. What does it do for the believer? Read Ephesians 6:16. **In addition to all this, take up the shield of faith, with which you can extinguish all the flaming arrows of the evil one.**

Satan is called the "accuser" (Revelation 12:10). One of his schemes is to drag believers down in guilt and shame, pointing out their failures. What are you feeling guilty about these days? Lied to your spouse? Blew your stack at the kids? Had an abortion? Skipped church? "Wimped out" on witnessing? Write your guilt causer(s) below.

☞ _____   ☞ _____

☞ _____   ☞ _____

Is this guilt from God or the accuser? If the guilt is leading you toward confession, correction and a release of the guilt, then it is the conviction of the Holy Spirit. If it is leading toward self-condemnation, discouragement and throwing in the towel, it is from the accuser. Don't be unaware of his schemes!

On the medieval shields, a family crest and motto were often affixed. What motto do you most need on your shield: FORGIVEN! LOVED! SAVED! CHILD OF GOD! Write one below.

FOCUS:
"I will praise you, O LORD, with all my heart." (Psalm 9:1)

What word is used most in Ephesians 6:18-20?

¹⁸And pray in the Spirit on all occasions with all kinds of prayers and requests. With this in mind, be alert and always keep on praying for all the saints.

¹⁹Pray also for me, that whenever I open my mouth, words may be given me so that I will fearlessly make known the mystery of the gospel, ²⁰for which I am an ambassador in chains. Pray that I may declare it fearlessly, as I should.

What is your first impulse when you think of prayer:

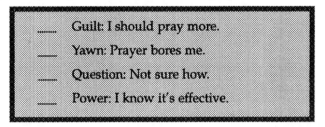

_____ Guilt: I should pray more.

_____ Yawn: Prayer bores me.

_____ Question: Not sure how.

_____ Power: I know it's effective.

What do verses 18-20 tell you about prayer? Write everything you can come up with.

_____

_____

_____

_____

_____

_____

If you struggle with giving prayer the importance Paul places on it, try viewing prayer as stepping on the accelerator. When you hit the gas, your effort is small, yet the power unleashed is great.

When you pray, your effort seems small, useless, ineffective. Yet you step on the pedal of power.

Jesus said, "Ask and you will receive." The opposite is true as well, "Ask not and you receive not." James wrote, **"You do not have, because you do not ask God."**

PRAYER:
Take a card and write the words "PRAY ABOUT IT" on the card. Put the card in your pocket, and whenever you touch it, pray about whatever is on your mind or around you, people, problems, places.

A FULL CUP

"Life Is Difficult"

"Life is difficult" is the opening line of a popular book. And a reality for many of us.

Contentment is difficult when life is difficult. When pests pervade.
Ants will continue to show up for your picnics uninvited.
Flies will ever collect on the screen door.
Starlings will never cease to dive bomb your newly washed car.
Roaches always find their way into your bathtub.
The mosquitoes will bite.   The gnats will circle.   The mice will gnaw.
Fleas will find the dog even when he doesn't leave a forwarding address.
Pests are from here to eternity.

But 'content-ment' does not have to do with the 'content' of your days.
Contentment does have to do with the content of your soul.
Contentment is not a matter of a carefree life.
Contentment is a matter of a careful faith.
Contentment does not arise from gaining perfect pest control.
Contentment arises from knowing the perfect Power who is in control.
It is realizing that all pests work for the good of those who love God.
Because God works for good. Because God works for you.
So nothing will be wasted.
Not one mosquito bite.   No rat's nest.
Not a single fly in the soup.

But being content doesn't mean you surrender. That you give in to the ever present pests. That you give up on pest control.
Contentment is not complacency.

Complacency says: I don't care. I give up.
Contentment says: I know God cares. I don't need to give up.

Complacency says: It doesn't really matter; it won't make any difference.
So why try?

Contentment says: Everything matters. Everything will be different.
So why quit?

Complacency is fatalism: what will happen will happen . . .

and it will probably be bad.

Contentment is faith-ism: what God wills will happen . . .

And it will certainly be good.

Pests need to be controlled, but pests never need control you nor your contentment.

Contentment is a gift from God.

And the pests are too small to carry that gift away.

MONDAY

FOCUS:
Lord, help reveal to me areas in my life where I am not content.

❑ Yes   ❑ No   Are you content?

❑ Yes   ❑ No   Are there areas in your life where you consistently dwell on the thought that you are being short-changed?

❑ Yes   ❑ No   Would others who know you well describe you as content?

What is the one major area of your life where you struggle with being content?

Don't rush ahead, fill in that box.

What are the character traits which caused you to develop this lack of contentment? Check those which apply.

___ Envy — comparing with others and always coming up short

___ Materialism — thinking that thrill comes through things

___ Perfectionism — anything less is the pits

___ Living in the past — looking back more often than ahead

___ Unforgiveness — picking at old scabs, pulling at new stitches

___ Insecurity — shrinking back because you already feel small

___ Worry — feeling certain tomorrow will be worse than today

Each of the above attitudes tends to take our eyes off God and onto our problems or other people. Read Psalm 37:1-8 and list at least seven ways David directs us to relate to the Lord.

¹Do not fret because of evil men
   or be envious of those who do wrong;
²for like the grass they will soon wither,
   like green plants they will soon die away.

³Trust in the LORD and do good;
   dwell in the land and enjoy safe pasture.
⁴Delight yourself in the LORD
   and he will give you the desires of your heart.

⁵Commit your way to the LORD;
   trust in him and he will do this:
⁶He will make your righteousness shine like the dawn,
   the justice of your cause like the noonday sun.

⁷Be still before the LORD and wait patiently for him;
   do not fret when men succeed in their ways,
   when they carry out their wicked schemes.

⁸Refrain from anger and turn from wrath;
   do not fret—it leads only to evil.

> _____
> _____
> _____
> _____
> _____
> _____
> _____

What is keeping you from doing these things?

_____
_____
_____

PRAYER:
Lord, will you reveal the things I allow to come between you and me? Give me the strength to tear down those self-imposed walls and come before you.

TUESDAY

FOCUS:
Dear Lord, teach me how to be content in You.

What is something you have learned to do in the past year? Surf the web? Use a cell phone? Drive a stick shift? What?

_____

_____

We are constantly learning, but have you ever considered that you need to learn how to be content? Read Philippians 4:11-13

> ¹¹I am not saying this because I am in need, for I have learned to be content whatever the circumstances. ¹²I know what it is to be in need, and I know what it is to have plenty. I have learned the secret of being content in any and every situation, whether well fed or hungry, whether living in plenty or in want. ¹³I can do everything through him who gives me strength.

Notice that the apostle Paul, maybe the greatest Christian of all time, admits that he had to learn how to be content whatever the circumstances. That is true contentment — when your circumstances do not control your emotions.

What circumstances tend to ruin your contentment?

____ Upset relationships   ____ Minor frustrations

____ Work difficulties   ____ Bad weather

____ Money problems   ____ Personal defeat

____ Physical pain   ____ Busy-ness

____ Unforeseen complications   ____ Delays

        ____ All of the above

For most of us, to say that we have learned to be content whatever the circumstances would seem to be nearly impossible. And yet Paul said that he has learned the secret. Write in your own words what Paul said is the secret.

_____

PRAYER:
Lord, help me to look past my circumstances to You.

FOCUS:
Continue, Lord, to reveal Yourself as the source of my contentment.

List the two sins of which God accuses His people in Jeremiah 2:13.

My people have committed two sins:
They have forsaken me,
    the spring of living water,
and have dug their own cisterns,
    broken cisterns that cannot hold water.

1.

2.

In this very symbolic passage, God communicates our tendency to look to ourselves and others for refreshment (contentment) instead of to Him. Why do you think we do that so often? Try to come up with three reasons.

✡ _____

✡ _____

✡ _____

Read John 4:13-14 and 7:37-39.

[13]Jesus answered, "Everyone who drinks this water will be thirsty again, [14]but whoever drinks the water I give him will never thirst. Indeed, the water I give him will become in him a spring of water welling up to eternal life."
[37]On the last and greatest day of the Feast, Jesus stood and said in a loud voice, "If anyone is thirsty, let him come to me and drink. [38]Whoever believes in me, as the Scripture has said, streams of living water will flow from within him." [39]By this he meant the Spirit, whom those who believed in him were later to receive. Up to that time the Spirit had not been given, since Jesus had not yet been glorified.

In these verses, who or what is the "living water?"

What is promised in this passage?

✝ _____

✝ _____

✝ _____

Have you drunk from the "spring of living water" recently?

❏ Often   ❏ Occasionally   ❏ Some time ago   ❏ I guess not

Will you do so now?   ❏ Yes   ❏ No

PRAYER:
Thank You, Lord, for being an eternal source of contentment.

THURSDAY

FOCUS:
Pray for someone who is currently going through extremely difficult circumstances.

Into every life, suffering will come. We don't like it, but it is as inevitable as crabgrass. Jesus said, **"In this world you will have trouble"** (John 16:33). We try to avoid pain and suffering, but we can't dodge it for a lifetime. What do we do in the midst of our own severe suffering, or how do we help a friend who is hurting badly?

What does Peter recommend that we do in 1 Peter 5:6-7? **⁶Humble yourselves, therefore, under God's mighty hand, that he may lift you up in due time. ⁷Cast all your anxiety on him because he cares for you.**

_____

What about God should cause us to take our anxieties to Him?

_____

_____

_____

_____

Galatians 6:2 says: **Carry each other's burdens, and in this way you will fulfill the law of Christ.** Whose burdens do you need to help carry today?

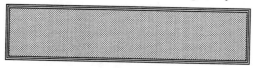

How do you plan to do so? Be specific.

Plan A: _____

_____

Plan B: _____

_____

Paul said that helping someone with their burdens, even if that is simply sorrowing with them over a loss, is literally fulfilling the law of Christ. Conclude today by reading John 13:34-35.

³⁴"A new command I give you: Love one another. As I have loved you, so you must love one another. ³⁵By this all men will know that you are my disciples, if you love one another."

What an opportunity you have today to allow others to know who you are by what you do!

PRAYER:
Dear Lord, give me the boldness to share someone's burdens in Your name.

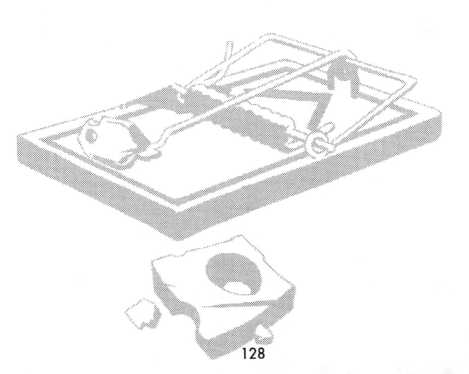

FRIDAY

FOCUS:
Lord, help me to be truly content in You today.

Contentment has nothing to do with getting what you want; it has every-thing to do with wanting what you have.

Contentment has to do with concentration. Your heart will follow your eyes. He who sees all he has is satisfied. He who sees only what others have lives disgruntled. What have your eyes been locked in upon lately?

_____

What has that focus done to your contentment?

❏ increased it   ❏ limited it   ❏ destroyed it

What do we have that Hebrews 12:1-3 encourages us to lock onto?

> [1]Therefore, since we are surrounded by such a great cloud of witnesses, let us throw off everything that hinders and the sin that so easily entangles, and let us run with perseverance the race marked out for us. [2]Let us fix our eyes on Jesus, the author and perfecter of our faith, who for the joy set before him endured the cross, scorning its shame, and sat down at the right hand of the throne of God. [3]Consider him who endured such opposition from sinful men, so that you will not grow weary and lose heart.

An Olympic runner eliminates any clothing that might slow his or her performance. If you doubt that, check their uniforms. Clothes are not bad in and of themselves. They are only bad during the race. Is there any "good clothing" that is taking your eyes off your "Contentment," Jesus? The heavy coat of a demanding job? The long necklace of an enticing rela-tionship? The wool pants of your many investments? What?

_____

Runners also tie their shoes, leap hurdles, stay on the path and out of the bushes. Shoelaces, hurdles and bushes are always bad things to get entangled in. What sin has been tripping you up?

_____

Read Hebrews 12:1-3 again. If you truly lived out these three verses, how would you be different?

_____

_____

_____

_____

Would you be content?

 PRAYER:
Write a prayer to close out this study book, thanking God for all He has taught you; rejoicing that He is not done yet.

Dear God,

Your pests may not be fully eliminated, but at least a few of your worst insects are identified, pinned, and labeled.

Your basement has less cobwebs;

Your garage, smaller mice;

Your pantry, fewer flies.

Congratulations.

You are well on your way to being pest free.